K9 Fraud!
Fraudulent Handling of Police Search Dogs
By Dr. Resi Gerritsen & Ruud Haak

Calgary, Alberta, Canada

© 2010 Resi Gerritsen & Ruud Haak

Library and Archives Canada Cataloguing in Publication

Gerritsen, Resi
  K9 fraud! : Fraudulent handling of police search dogs / Resi Gerritsen, Ruud Haak.

Includes bibliographical references and index.
ISBN 978-1-55059-393-8

1. Police dogs--Training. 2. Search dogs--Training. 3. Police witnesses. I. Haak, Ruud II. Title.
HV8025.G47 2010   363.25'2   C2010-903686-7

Detselig Enterprises Ltd.
210 1220 Kensington Rd NW
Calgary, Alberta T2N 3P5
www.temerondetselig.com
temeron@telusplanet.net
p. 403-283-0900 f. 403-283-6947

All rights reserved. No part of this book may be reproduced in any form or by any means without permission in writing from the publisher.

We acknowledge the financial support of the Alberta Foundation for the Arts for our publishing program.

SAN: 113-0234
ISBN: 978-1-55059-393-8
Printed In Canada.
Cover design by James Dangerous.

COMMITTED TO THE DEVELOPMENT OF CULTURE AND THE ARTS

Table of Contents

Chapter 1: Fraud with Scent Identification Line-Ups • 11

First Suspect Discriminations • 11
Scent Identifications • 13
Discriminating Similar Odors • 16
Special Bikes • 18
Knowing the Suspect • 19
Influencing the Dog • 20
Inadvertent Signal • 22
Correct the Dog • 23
Fitting-room Murder Case • 24
Police Dog – Tim • 24

Three Failures • 25
The New Protocol • 26
Importance of the Helper • 28
Deventer Murder Case • 29
Perjury and Forgery • 31
'Junk Science' • 31
A Lot of Faults • 32
Uses in Criminal Cases • 33
International Standards • 36

Chapter 2: Dogs' Responsiveness to Human Gestures • 39

Clever Hans Effect • 39
A Miraculous Horse • 40
Subtle Movements • 41
Clever Dog Nora • 42
Test with Signs • 42

Glancing Cues • 44
Pointing Gestures • 45
The Detour Test • 47
Working Blind • 49

Chapter 3: Fraud with Tracking Dogs • 51

Historical Tracking Dogs • 53
Night Watchmen • 55
Police Tracking Dogs • 58
Dog-Detectives • 59
Other Miraculous Stories • 61
Bold Dog Handlers • 66
Incorrect Human Interpretations • 66
Putting Pressure on the Suspect • 67
Influencing by the handler • 69
Many Excesses • 70
Poor Results • 71
Training Method • 72
Dog Handler Larry Harris (1) • 74
Dog Handler Larry Harris (2) • 75
Signs of the Handler • 78
Deliberately • 78
Dog Handler John Preston • 79

Chapter 4: Scent Research and Tracking Experiments • 83

Human World • 83
Dog World • 84
Different Worlds • 85
Prickle Thresholds • 85
Various Levels • 87
Perception • 88
Tiredness • 88
Prickle Summarizing • 89
Systematic Training • 90
Lost Knowledge • 91
The First Tracking Tests • 92
Systematically Research • 93
Most's Tracking Cross • 94
Repeating the Tests • 95
Disagreements • 96
Extensive Experiments • 97
Control Test • 97
Air-transferred Odor • 98
Drops of saps • 100
Tracks without Human Odor • 100
Clean-scent Tracking • 101
Influence of Fatty Acids • 102
Y-scheme Tracks • 103
Breathing and Scanning Odors • 104
Sniffing • 107
Direction of the Track • 108

Chapter 5: Fraud with Mantrailing • 111

Old Times Revive • 113
The Jeffrey Allen Grant Case • 114
The Anthrax Letters • 115
The Scott Peterson Case • 118
Stupid Utterances • 119
Dog Handler Sandra Anderson • 120
Dog Handler Penny Bell • 122
Dog Handler Keith Pikett (1) • 123
Dog Handler Keith Pikett (2) • 124
What is Mantrailing? • 125
What Can't Mantrailers Do? • 128
The Scent Article Method Project • 129
Bloodhounds – Tracking/Trailing • 130
Five Big Mistakes in Mantrailing • 130
The Joshua Wade Case • 135

Chapter 6: Human Odor and Dog's Scent Perception • 139

Scents of the Track • 139
Human Odor in the Track • 143
Scents of the Trail • 145
Individual Human Odor • 146
Influencing Odors • 146
Body Openings • 146
Human Skin • 146
Skin Glands • 148
Odor Production • 150
Stability of Odor • 153
Dog's Scent Perception • 155
Inside the Dog's Nose • 155
Odor Contacts Receptor • 158
From Nose to Brain • 160
Brain Cortex vs. Limbic System • 162

Chapter 7: Scent Problems and Training Problems • 165

Problems in the Olfactory Organ • 165
Odor and Odorless • 166
Temperature and Scent • 168
Alternating Perception • 168
Smelling Problems • 169
Adaptation and Nose-fatigue • 171
Chemical Blockers • 173
Scent and Memory • 174
Failure Scents • 175
Females' Sensitive Sense • 176
Amount of Scent • 176
Complex Scents • 177
Extremely Strenuous • 178
Serious Problems • 179
Motivation • 181
Systematic Mistakes • 181
Handling Mistakes • 182
'Shape' and 'Content' Problems • 183
Reading The Dog • 184
Training Advice • 185

Chapter 8: Avoiding and Preventing Fraud • 187

Scent Identification Line-Ups • 187
1. Unintentional fraud • 189
Negligent treatment • 189
Not keeping to the protocol • 189

Management Attention • 189
2. Intentional fraud • 191
Intentionally work up to a certain result • 191
Financial benefit • 192
Faster or easier 'solved' cases • 192
Disguise characteristics of the dog • 192
Become known in the media • 192
Being a better dog handler then others • 192

An Explosive Case • 193
3. Civilians in Crimal Investigations • 193
Is their help necessary or do they intrude? • 194
Civilian dogs certified by correct standards? • 194
A missing persons case can become a crime • 194
Prepared to recognize certain traces of crime? • 194

Shady Evidence • *195*
4. Contamination of scents • *196*
Dual-purpose trained dogs • *196*
Keep and use scent and objects clean • *196*
Clean-scent training • *197*

Making Impossible Possible • *197*
5. Improper training • *199*
Easy scoring by using tracks • *199*
Selection of starting material • *200*
The team: handler and dog • *201*
Unsuitable dog for the task • *202*
Use of an incorrect training method • *203*
Too fast to get results • *203*
Dog's physical, mental and search condition • *203*
Are the examination requirements realistic? • *204*

Insurance Fraud • *205*
6. Unfamiliar influences on dogs • *205*
Handlers, instructors, helpers and spectators • *205*
Training 'controlled' or really 'blind'? • *206*

Bibliography • *209*

About the Authors • *213*

Introduction:

Why and how does one commit police dog fraud?

Fraud by definition means 'treacherousness' or 'deceit.' In regards to regulation and protocol of judicial and forensic investigation, the foreknowledge of working towards a certain result dispite whatever the truth may contain is an act of fraudulent investigation. Therefore, committing fraud 'on oath' or in an 'official report' is inexcusable; however, why do police dog handlers commit fraud? Here are some important reasons, which will be comprehensively discussed in this book.

1. Lack of knowledge about what influences a dog.
2. Shortage of skills to train the dog in the right way.
3. In order to disguise the quality or characteristics of the dog.
4. In order to solve a case quickly.
5. In order to financially benefit from it.
6. In order to be a better dog handler than others.

In this book we will consider at length fraud within police search dogs, giving lots of examples along the way. Our hope is that understanding fraud will become clearer after reading this book. We will discuss more than the miscarriages of justice; broken lives, and even those sentenced to death due to fraudulent investigations is absolutely unforgivable. Cases and causes of fraud in the past and present will be systematically discussed in many different types of police dog work. Such as, police search dogs that perform scent identification line-ups, tracking and mantrailing. In the final chapter we will discuss the possibilities of avoiding fraud with police search dogs.

Dr. Resi Gerritsen and Ruud Haak.

Chapter 1:
Fraud with Scent Identification Line-Ups

"Thousands of Dutch police scent identification tests now void," was the headline in all the newspapers across The Netherlands in 2006. In the article, the Board of Attorney General wrote a letter to public prosecutors stating, *"All scent identification line-ups which took place after 1997 by police dogs in the regions of North and East Netherlands, may not be used as evidence in criminal trials."*

IN OCTOBER 2006, two police dog handlers from the division of North and East Netherlands admitted to a court in the Dutch town of Leeuwarden, that they hadn't been perfoming the scent identification line-ups according to the rules. In a number of suspect line-ups, the handlers knew beforehand which suspect was carrying the particular odor found at the crime. After this testimony, the court immediately acquitted the case, and the National Department of Criminal Investigation made an inquiry of all the district's seven police dog handlers. Who were then removed from office.

First Suspect Discriminations

Since the beginning of the twentieth century, scent identification line-ups have been extensively used by police forces in Europe. In such line-ups, specially trained police dogs compare the corpus delicti – the human scent on an object found at a crime scene – with the odor of a suspect. As early as 1910, Friedo Schmidt from Stralsund, Germany, wrote in his book about the way these corpus delicti should be saved and stored:

'By no means should the article be left at the scene of the crime or be taken by hand by the criminal investigator. This must become common knowledge to every man working at a crime scene. The article must not be wrapped in paper or packed in a wooden or cardboard box, because it will take on the odor of the foreign material. I suggest glass containers as the best means of storage, for glass is an inert material. Substances like sweat and blood incur no changes when in contact with glass. Every article must be separate and, size permitting, must be put in a sealable glass-receptacle equipped with a glass-stopper. Such containers have the advantage of transparency, so the article, for instance a handkerchief, can easily pass from hand to hand and important details, such as a monogram, can also be observed whilst in the receptacle.'

The first milestone in suspect identification with dogs cannot be mentioned without Inspector Bussenius from Braunschweig, Germany. He was the champion of police dog handling at the time, and a formidable dog trainer. His successful work with police dogs provided authorities with key victories in the support the police dog movement. In particular, the use of his German Shepherd, *Harras von der Polizei*, in the Duwe murder case at Hagenhof – a farm outside of Braunschweig. June 1903, Inspector Bussenius and Harras von der Polizei proved to the world for the first time the value of dogs in the investigation of homicide cases. Their success in the Duwe case is often seen as a turning point in the history of police dogs.

In 1911, Dr. Friedo Schmidt wrote about this case:

'June 3 1903, an eleven-year-old girl was killed at the Hagenhof farm in the German village of Königslutter near Braunschweig. The forensic research team could not come up with evidence although one of the farmhands was suspected of the murder. After days of continuous but fruitless investigation, the public prosecutor asked Inspector Bussenius from Braunschweig to find the murderer with his German Shepherd, 'Harras von der Polizei.' Upon their arrival at the Hagenhof farm – four days after the homicide – all twelve employees of the farm were placed in a line in the yard. After that Harras was brought to the crime scene, where he was commanded to sniff the bloodstains and the surrounding area. The dog immediately picked up the track. First, he briefly scanned one of the forensic investigators who had visited the crime scene earlier, but before long the dog left him and continued tracking. The dog then sniffed each person standing in the line, one after the other. Suddenly when he reached the eighth person in line, Harras hurled himself at the man who cried out loudly in protest. The accused man was the suspected farmhand Duwe. The test was repeated two more times. Each time, the people in the line changed positions, but the result was the same: Harras lunged himself ferociously at Duwe, paying no attention to the other farmhands. After that Duwe was arrested. At first, Duwe tried to deny the murder, but soon he made a full confession. Duwe was condemned to death.'

Scent Identifications

The first scent identification conducted by the Dutch took place in 1914. Officer Jacob Water of the Amsterdam police and his dog 'Albert,' a fawn longhaired Belgian Shepherd Dog, traveled all over the Netherlands following the tracks of suspects. The work done with Albert was impressive, and later became the foundation for scent identification line-ups in

Albert, the fawn longhaired Belgian Sheep Dog of Officer Jacob Water of the Amsterdam police in 1914.

the Netherlands, and of search dogs in general. One case involved the director of a milk factory whose throat was cut with a razor. A cap and a razor were found in the factory, near the spot where the man was killed. Officer Water wrote about this case in his memoirs:

> 'When first assigned to the case, Albert was given the razor for odor detection and later on, the cap. He tracked the scent throughout the factory, then outside to a tree where the murderer had probably mounted a bicycle and left the scene. In the meantime, it was rumored that a man, who was not unknown to the police, had been seen in the vicinity of the factory. Almost three weeks later, this man was arrested; however, he denied being the murderer. Again Albert was asked for help. The suspect was placed in a circle together with other people. After sniffing at the razor, the dog pointed out the suspect without hesitation – who continued to deny involvement in the murder. So a second test was carried out. The caps of all those present were spread out on the ground along with the cap found in the factory. Albert sniffed at the suspect then went to the pile of caps. Soon he picked out a cap, but this was not the one found in the factory. After searching again Albert brought the cap found in the factory to his handler. The first cap belonged to the suspect: he was wearing it when he was arrested. Officer Water concluded that since this cap contained the strongest odor of the suspect, it was picked out by the dog first.'

Prof. Dr. F.J.J. Buytendijk, an expert of animal behavior, examined Albert's scenting ability. Six people were lined up. Each person took a pebble into his hand, and at a signal they all threw their pebble onto a path strewn with other pebbles. The dog was allowed to sniff the hands of one of the individuals, and then Mr. Water commanded Albert to search. He searched the path, sniffing intently at each of the pebbles thrown onto the path, until he reached the 'correct' pebble and retrieved it. Prof. Buytendijk wrote about that in his book:

> 'It was interesting to observe how the dog's behavior changed the moment he discovered the 'correct' pebble. Quietly searching from one spot to the

other, his ears suddenly stood on end, and with hastened movement, he used his nose and mouth to isolate the pebble from the rest and quickly retrieved it. The dog behaved in a totally different manner when he, either through the influence of his handler or other distractions, picked up a wrong pebble. In these cases the dog reacted in an uncertain, almost shy manner.'

Another case, in which Officer Water and Albert were involved, was the murder of the mayor in the Dutch town of Beesd. In the last year of the First World War a burglary took place in the town hall – the motive was to steal ration cards. A ladder was placed at the back of the building, reaching the first floor where a window was opened with a crowbar. The mayor, who was probably woken up by the noise, went into the town clerk's office to investigate and was shot dead. Officer Water wrote:

'At the crime scene Albert found the pistol and the crowbar. Three men loitering around the vicinity of Beesd were arrested for vagrancy and placed in a big circle between other suspects. Introduced to the scent on the crowbar, Albert pointed out one of the suspects by barking at him. Of course the suspect denied it, but was taken away by a gendarme. Again, Albert took the odor from the crowbar and returned to the circle of gathered men. He stopped in front of a humpback who, after been shown the pistol and the crowbar, conceded that the crowbar belonged to the person who had first been picked out by the dog.
"And the pistol?" he was asked.
"The pistol belongs to Mr. De Rijk, who left in the direction of the Belgian border," the man answered. A warrant for his arrest was immediately issued to all the border patrols.
"But what did you do?" the humpback was asked.
"Well," he said, "I laid a plank over a ditch and placed the ladder against the town hall." He was questioned about whether the first man, the owner of the crowbar, had anything to do with the affair, he answered: "Yes Sir. He forced the window open for Mr. De Rijk."

As a result of this testimony, the case was closed.'

Discriminating Similar Odors

Police arriving at the scene of the crime, 1918

In 1918, scent identification in the Netherlands was led by forensic-expert Dr. C.J. van Ledden Hulsebosch from Amsterdam. He described a number of cases in a book he wrote about his forty years as a police investigator. Some illustrated the precise manner of his work, as in the case of the 'murderer with manure.' In January 1918, Albert and Bob, Amsterdam's first two police dogs, had to solve another murder case by scent identification. Although this case did not deal with dogs using human scents, it illustrated the capability of dogs to discriminate between similar odors. Officer Jacob Water, who worked with the dogs, depicted the situation:

Chapter 1

Near the town of Breezand, a farmer was found dead. Based on some clues and fingerprints two people were suspected of the murder and arrested. The fingerprints of one of them were found at the crime scene and this person confessed. In his confession he explained how he and the other man had taken off their shoes and then climbed through a small window and thus gained entry to the barnyard. There they landed in a cowshed. The second suspect slipped, and his right foot landed in a manure trough. With his hand he wiped most of the manure off his sock. After the murder, he stepped back into his shoe with his soiled sock. Mr. Van Ledden Hulsebosch now wanted to examine these shoes. A gendarme went to the suspect's cell to fetch them. The suspect told the gendarme he had visited the cattle market in the town of Purmerend that Tuesday, where he had gotten cow manure on his sock. To a human nose, the manure of one cow smells much the same as another, so the dung was not necessarily incriminating; however, Mr. Van Ledden Hulsebosch felt differently. He believed dogs could distinguish manure from different cowsheds. Therefore he asked the gendarme from Breezand to bring him cow manure from twelve different cowsheds – including that where the murder had taken place – in twelve well-cleaned jam jars. The jam jars were numbered and a list was compiled of the owners of the cowsheds. Now, Mr. Van Ledden Hulsebosch took seventy two equal pieces of paper and divided them into six series, each numbered from one to twelve according to the numbers on the jam jars. Manure was spread on the numbered papers then these were distributed throughout the courtyard of the police headquarters, between shrubs and in all possible places. After this was done, the unique experiment began. Mr. Van Ledden Hulsebosch first wanted to test whether the dogs were able to find dung from a particular shed through 'sorting'. To do this I took one of the pieces of paper with manure, let the dogs smell it and commanded them to search. Immediately the dogs started searching around and soon they found all the papers with the same number. To exclude all coincidence, the test was repeated several times with other manure papers, all with the same result. This experiment proved that the dogs could indeed discriminate between the manure from different cowsheds. First, the dogs were presented the left shoe of the suspect and took scent. The dogs hesitated. Apparently they did not recognize the scent and they sniffed around listlessly. Then they were presented the right shoe, which had been the shoe stained with manure. Immediately their manner changed. They started wagging their tails and began searching. In no time, all the papers with the corresponding number to the jam jar containing the manure from murder scene were laid out before us. And as if a final conviction to guilty party, Albert brought the whole jam jar a few seconds later.'

Special Bikes

The 'sorting box' between the frame of a bicycle of the Amsterdam Police.

The 'sorting box' placed on the luggage carrier of the officer's bicycle.

In a report made by the Amsterdam police in 1930, special boxes were made for scent identification line-ups:

'Since objects used as evidence has to be kept strictly separate, but also must be transportable, we designed a 'sorting-box.' In practice, this has been a success. The box has two different transportation applications: one is to hang the box between the frame of a bicycle and the other is to place it on a luggage carrier. With these boxes, the evidence can be transported, and also kept for some time. However, it is necessary to ventilate the boxes after each use.'

Knowing the Suspect

In accordance with scientific development, the manner in which scent identifications line-ups are conducted, have changed over the years. The current standard operational protocol is the result of a history of rigorous scientific experiment, and experience. The changes in this protocol, occurring in the last century, illustrate these changing views and insights. In the 1920s and 1930s, the line-ups where the dogs made their choice consisted of an actual line-up of people, as described before. The object that contained the scent of the perpetrator, the corpus delicti, was kept in a self preserving-bottle. The suspect was made to stand in a row or circle together with a number of other people referred to as foils. The handler would let his dog smell the corpus delicti and the dog would then compare the scent on the object with that of the foils and suspect. The dog would then indicate a match by barking at that person. The row usually consisted of six people and the dog had to repeat his choice two or three times. The handler would often assume beforehand which suspect was guilty by the end of first test.

An obvious drawback of this style of line-up was that the subject, frightened at being considered the culprit, could react in such a manner that would influence the dog's choice. The dog could choose someone based on this behavior instead of on the scent.

In later years, the foils were replaced by objects. A number of people were asked to put something that belonged to them in a row on the ground. It was not known which object belonged to whom. The corpus delicti was still kept in the preserving-bottle. The handler would let his dog smell at the corpus delicti and the dog would retrieve the object with the matching human scent. If an object belonging to the suspect was matched, it would be placed in another position within the row and the dog would repeat his choice a second or third time. Then

A scent identification line-up on worn shoes, ca. 1950.

the handler would know which object belonged to the culprit!

Influencing the Dog

In 1932, Prof. Buytendijk wrote in his book a clear warning about the foreknowledge a police dog handler has about a certain suspect when carrying out a scent line-up:

> 'It is necessary that all tests are performed in such a way that the dog by itself is influenced by the evidence, while excluding the handler. Also, it is recommended to let the dog choose between similar objects. Once I saw a scent identification test that obviously succeeded, but was absolutely incorrect in its execution. May the report be a warning to ensure the

Chapter 1

In order to prevent direct contact with the dog in the man-line-up system, the men were made to stand behind a screen (Police Rotterdam, ca. 1970).

objective in the use of police dogs: A coat was found at a crime scene, and the investigators wanted a detained suspect to admit that the coat belonged to him. Six coats were lined-up in a court yard, one of which was the coat from the crime scene and the other five belonged to the officers. After the police dog had been allowed to take the scent of the suspect he retrieved the corpus delicti. Such a test doesn't prove anything. Of course, the coat found at the crime scene was a totally different type odor than the coats belonging to the officers. Imagine that the odors were visible; in this case, the dog would have seen five gray coats and a single red one, so it is obvious that the dog would retrieve the one which was completely different than the others. Only if all objects belonged to the same type of odor, and were optically identical in measurement and form, could there be a chance of obtaining reliable results. Even more dangerous is to let a dog choose a person from a line-up of men based on the odor of an object – even when the handler doesn't know the test or hasn't any suspicion of a particular suspect – because there always will be a good chance that the dog will react to the slightest movement of one of the men in line.'

In later variants of the man-line-up system the men were made to stand behind a screen to prevent direct contact with the dog. Later still, fans were placed behind the suspects to blow their scent straight through the screen.

Inadvertent Signal

But even after the line-up of men was changed to a row of objects, problems occurred. It became obvious that dogs preferred retrieving certain types of objects to others and that the line-up were, therefore, not objective. So in the 1950s, *similar* objects were used in the row. Keys were chosen as a standard object, since in the earlier years, keys had been often used, and the dogs had ample experience with them. Identical keys were cleaned in boiling water, and handed out to a number of people including the suspect to hold in their pockets or hands. These keys were then placed in paper envelopes or preserving-bottles until the actual scent identification line-up was performed. The dog was given the scent of the corpus delicti and had to retrieve the matching key a number of times. Each time the same keys were rearranged in the row.

Further changes in Dutch scent line-up procedures were made during the 1960s. The corpus delicti was preserved in modern plastic, while keys were replaced by aluminum tubes, usually engraved with a number; however, the aluminum tubes proved to be too soft and were easily damaged by the dogs chewing them. Later they were replaced by stainless steel tubes, which are still used today. The method in the 1960s was that three people held two tubes each in their pockets, then these tubes served as foils in the row. The suspects were asked to hold three or four tubes. If a suspect was unwilling to hold the tubes, the tubes were scented in the armpits of their jacket. For the Rotterdam police, this was the standard method to obtain the scent of a suspect. The row was composed of six or seven tubes from which the dog had to choose after having smelled the corpus delicti. This was repeated a number of times using a fresh tube with the suspect's scent each time; the same foil tubes were used over and over again. The handler usually knew the position of the suspect's tube, but a number of them preferred not to know so as not to inadvertently signal its location to the dog.

Correct the Dog

1968, in the Dutch village of Oirschot, a scent identification line-up played an important role in a court case concerning the murder of a pub-owner. The suspect was a vagrant. The vagrant and a number of other people had all provided their scent on a number of tubes by holding them in their hands. These tubes were used for the line-up and put into a row. The handler who conducted the line-up knew which of the tubes had belonged to the vagrant. When he saw his dog intended to retrieve a tube that was scented by one of the others, he corrected his dog verbally. The dog continued to search, and next retrieved the tube that had been scented by the vagrant.

The newspapers discussed the court case: all of the evidence, including the scent identification line-up, was critically examined and the suspect was acquitted twice. An important part of the discussion concerned the handler's prior knowledge of the position of the tube scented by the vagrant. Although most people agreed that it would be better had the handler not have the foreknowledge during the line-up, they did not really seem aware of the consequences of the situation. It is possible that a dog reacts to signals that the handler is unaware of. A slight catching of breath or the relaxation of muscles once the dog is paying attention to the 'correct' tube can be made involuntarily and unconsciously. If a handler systematically reacts in this way, the dog can use this signal as a way to being rewarded for choosing 'correctly.'

Fitting-room Murder Case

In the 1980s, again the scent identification line-up came under fire in the courts, in a famous case that was known as the 'Paskamermoord' ('Fitting-room murder'). On Friday November 30 1984, a customer found the twenty-year-old shop assistant, Sandra van Raalten, dead in a fitting-room of a clothing boutique in the town of Zaanstad. It was a particularly bloody murder, the girl had been gagged with a handkerchief, her hands and feet had been bound with strips from the fitting room curtain, and her throat had been cut. She was found in a big pool of her own blood. The blood was also splattered on the walls of the fitting-room. Although roughly 250 Dutch Notes were missing in the cash register, just as jewelry of Sandra was missing, the police didn't believe the motive was robbery. "When robbing, an attacker wouldn't take great pains over gag and binding a victim," the police said. In an autopsy, they concluded that no signs of sexual contact were found and forensic investigators found no marks of the perpetrator. The motive of the murder remained unclear.

Police Dog – Tim

The brutal murder attracted a lot of attention from the press, and the police invested about thirty men on the case, but without any progress. The investigations did not lead to results – just a lot of loose ends and people contradicting each other. Two years later, another team of investigators took over the case and a suspicion finally led them to a friend of Sandra, and then to a thirty three-years-old local

Chapter 1

Police Dog 'Tim' working out a scent identification line-up – as seen here on a rubber mat in a hall of the police courtyard. (Police Zaanstad, 1985)

bicycle dealer Rob van Zaane. In 1986, two scent identification line-ups were performed with the bicycle dealer as the suspect. In one line-up his handkerchief was used then, ten days later, the strip of curtain used to tie the girl's ankles and wrists were used. The same police dog, 'Tim,' was used for both line-ups and in both line-ups the bicycle dealer was pointed out. In the first trial, the bicycle dealer was convicted to twelve years in prison based heavily on the evidence found from the line-ups. He said it was possible he had given the handkerchief to the girl the evening before, but had given an earlier statement that he never had a handkerchief with him, this was not considered credible.

Three Failures

Another defense lawyer took over, and the scent identification line-ups were re-examined. A number of experts were called in, and three major flaws were found.

First, the quality of the dog was in discussion. The dog, 'Tim,' who was used for the line-ups, was a trained narcotics dog. This was considered to be a disadvantage as it is better to have single-purpose dog.

Secondly, the quality of the objects used for the line-ups were discussed. Both the handkerchief and the strip of curtain were contaminated with blood and possibly the corpse's odor; they also had not been preserved properly. They also may have been 'too old,' considering that the line-ups were conducted almost two years after the crime had been committed.

Thirdly, the handler knew which position in the line-up the tube that had the bicycle dealer's scent was.

The appeal case was a dramatic one. The scent identification line-up was disqualified, the police investigators were accused of being biased against the bicycle dealer and a number of loose ends in the investigation became blatantly apparent. The bicycle dealer was acquitted, but the police and members of the public prosecution remained convinced of his guilt. In 2001, the murder was finally solved. Improved DNA techniques made it possible to match DNA found at the crime scene to a man who, at the time, had been regarded as a possible suspect. He had been interrogated during the investigation, but the police let him go due to lack of evidence. This man, a drug addict and a notorious thief, had already died in hospital in 1992. The 'cold case' team accepted the possibility that the handkerchief could have belonged to the bicycle dealer. Nevertheless, Rob van Zaane felt the relief of finally being clear of suspicion.

The New Protocol

As a consequence of all those faults of the past, and after critical scientific review by Dr. Adee Schoon of the University of Leiden, in 1997, a new protocol to Dutch scent identification line-ups was introduced. In this protocol, a police officer as a 'certified helper' prepares the test and places the stainless steel tubes in two rows on two platforms. The dog handler and the dog are absent during the preparation of the line-up. The handler does not know the position of the different scents and, all officers involved testify to a verbal agreement, which is apart the official report written under an oath of office.

In this protocol, the odor of the suspect is one of seven different odors. Each

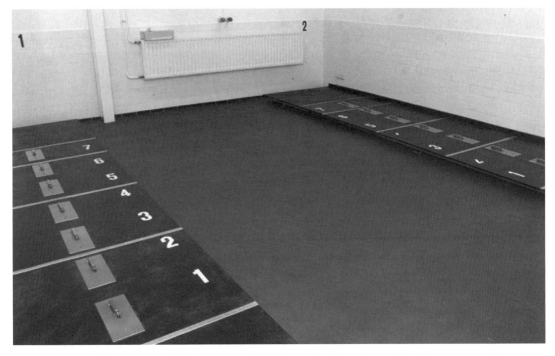

The scent identification room which contains two platforms, each with seven stainless steel scent carriers. (KLPD, 2002).

of these seven odors is present in two rows, but in a different sequence. Five of the odors in both rows are from foils. The seventh odor belongs to a control person. The position of the odors is random. The handler does not know which odors belong to the suspect or the control person or foil.

Before the dog is allowed to compare the odor of the corpus delicti with the odors in the rows, the ability of the dog to perform a scent identification line-up is tested. The dog must first search for the scent of the control person in both rows. By doing this, the dog also shows that it has no preference or special interest for the odor of the suspect. Only after positively identifying the control person in both rows, may the dog compare the odor of the corpus delicti with the remaining six odors. If the dog responds to the odor of the suspect and ignores all the other odors, this is considered a 'positive identification'.

Importance of the Helper

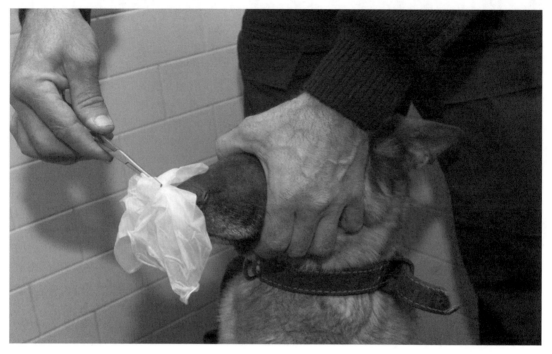

Letting the dog smell the odor of the perpetrator on an object. (KLPD, 2002).

Foreknowledge of which tube has the scent of the suspect clearly gives too many possibilities for manipulation of the objectivity of the experiment. It is absolutely necessary for the handler to have no predisposition of which odor is where. Therefore the 'certified helper' must prepare the test in absence of dog and handler. The most common method is to present the stainless steel tubes on a platform where they can be clamped into place. These scent carriers are presented according to one of thirty six different sequences, which are coded by two figures (each figure between one and six). The sequence is determined by the helper, who chooses at random, usually with assistance of a six-sided die. The helper installs the scent-carriers in two rows according to this sequence, which is also in accordance to the standard presentation method. As soon as the dog responses to a scent – each dog reacting in their own unique manner, whether it is biting, scratching, etc. – the handler signals the helper. After a correct response the dog is given a reward. The most common reward is that, by pressing a button, the helper releases the matching stainless steel tube from the platform, so that the dog can retrieve it.

If the dog responds to a smell that does not match the suspect, the handler signals and the dog is disqualified – the test stops. This disqualification is reported and mentioned in official reports. If the dog does not respond to any of the odors, after smelling all the tubes, the handler recalls the dog. This is also a disqualification. Also, if the dog does not work systematically, and as a result misses one or more of the tubes, the dog is disqualified. With the many ways that a scent identification line-up can go wrong, the work of the helper has to be done very carefully, and with a great sense of responsibility.

Deventer Murder Case

This leads us to the beginning of the chapter, when the Board of Attorney General was cited saying:

> "All scent identification line-ups which took place after 1997 by police dogs in the regions of North and East Netherlands, may not be used as evidence in criminal trials."

This occured during the 'Deventer Murder Case' in November 2006. Before, in 1999, the murder of Jacqueline Wittenberg – an old rich widow, in the Dutch town of Deventer – was initially believed to be solved with the help of a scent identification line-up. Her murderer was obviously someone she knew, because she never admitted strangers into her home. Even for people she knew, she only admitted them if she knew beforehand they were arriving. So when she was found murdered, but no signs of breaking and entering were found, the group of suspects was immediately limited. The most obvious suspect was her tax specialist Ernest Louwes, the executer of her recent will. He was president of the foundation that received her money, the bank account of this foundation was in his name, and he had spent her money for private matters, which was contrary to her wishes. He had a key to her house and was a regular guest. No murder weapon was found on the premises; however, a knife was discovered two days later nearby her home, under a porch. It was moved indoors by the neighbor who prevented touching it with his bare hands by covering his hand with his sleeve. No blood was found on the knife. Later, scent identification was done using this knife and the dog pointed out Ernest Louwes. This identification was performed according to the new 1997 regulations; first two trials to establish the capability of the dog, followed by two trials where the dog matched the odor on the knife to the odor of the suspect.

The suspect admitted having visited her in the morning, but continued to deny a later visit and the murder. However, a telephone call record showed a call had been made from his mobile telephone to her house shortly before the murder – a call lasting 16 seconds. This fitted into the pattern of calling just before arriving, as was customary with the old lady. Mobile telephones use telecom antennae, distributed all over the country to form a telephone network. Telephone records also show which antenna is used for each call – the one nearest to the caller. In this case, the call went through the telecom antennae in Deventer. Again, this fitted into the pattern of calling just before arriving. The suspect admitted to the call, but denied having been in the neighborhood. He said he was some twenty five kilometers away from her town. A telecom expert testified that if the call had been made from the place the suspect claimed he had been, it wouldn't have gone through the antennae it did. The suspect could not have been where he claimed – he was where he made the call. The suspect continued to deny everything.

In the lower courts he was acquitted, due to lack of sufficient evidence. In an appeal in 2000, court experts testified in detail about evidence including the mobile telephone network and the scent identification line-ups, and he was convicted to twelve years in prison for the crime. Two years later, in 2002, the Supreme Court of the Netherlands concluded that *"the knife used in the scent identification line-up could not be the murder weapon."*

Chapter 1

Perjury and Forgery

The seven police dog handlers of North and East Netherlands region were prosecuted for perjury and forgery, because it was found that they hadn't performed the scent identification line-ups *exactly* in accordance to the regulations. According to these rules, the dog handler may not know the position of the scent carriers of the suspect, to avoid influencing his dog. This step was found to be omitted in many cases between September 1997 and March 2006. Even worse, was that the official reports stated that all identification line-ups were processed in compliance with the standard codes of operation. In November 2007, the seven police dog handlers were convicted to penal labor of 240 hours. Six of the seven handlers were also incarcerated for two years and were removed entirely from their position. Only the dog handler that had shed light on situation was allowed to continue his duty.

'Junk Science'

In sharp contrast with the Netherlands, where there exists a validated protocol complete with strict rules, in the United States there are no such standard and procedure for a scent identification line-up. Each dog handler makes a line-up in the manner that they seem fit. This is a situation that leads to lots of mistakes, and also fraud.

Ed Lavandera of CNN said in 2009, the Innocence Project of Texas (IPOT) calls the practice of scent identification line-ups by dogs as a forensic tool a 'junk science that's being used by prosecutors and judges to convict people.' The nonprofit group, which is dedicated to discovering and overturning wrongful convictions, wants state governments to ban the use of scent identification line-ups. They state an unknown number of people have been wrongly accused or convicted from the dog-scent line-ups. Some of these we will discuss in the next chapters.

In the United States, the most common technique for a scent identification line-up is: a police investigator aquires the scent of the suspect, and foils by rubbing a gauze pad on their body or clothes. In the line-up these gauze pads are placed into tin cans. The cans are placed at a distance of three to four meters, in a row in an open area. The handler gives the dog the scent of the corpus delicti, packed in a plastic bag, and then the handler and dog, on leash, walk down the line of tin cans. If the dog matches the scent, the dog will give a sign. After that the tin can is place in another sequence, and again handler and dog walk along the line of tin cans.

A Lot of Faults

Beside the possibilities of fraud, in such a procedure a lot of faults become transparent:

- In this line-up procedure there is no 'controlled line-up' in order to check the general working ability of the dog. A dog can perform poorly due to a number of reasons, either physical or motivational. Checking the dog's ability to perform immediately before the real comparison leads to the exclusion of dogs that do not work well and this increases the reliability of the outcome of the line-up.

- This procedure has no control on the attractiveness of an odor to the dog. In European procedures, this control is generally done by letting the suspect be a foil in the 'controlled line-up' where the dog has to smell, and ignore, the odor of the suspect. This proves there is nothing especially attracting in the suspects odor.

- The scent of the corpus delicti, like those of the suspect and the foils, need to be collected in a proper manner. The best method of preservation is handling all objects with a pair of well-cleaned tongues and placing it into a clean glass jar with a twist-off top. Subsequently, it needs to be registered, stored and transported properly.

- Are all the foils selected similar the suspect, or do they differ? Foils should be of the same sex, race and age, with consideration of when their odor was selected.

- The tins, most of the time, are not well cleaned before use – which causes contamination of odors. Tins should be either sterilized in a stove, or washed with soap in a dishwasher prior to being boiled in clean water.

- The plastic bags used to pack the gauzes are usually placed by police officers with their bare hands. This procedure can cause contamination of odors that confuses the dog in his decission.

- By placing the tins outside in a park or another outdoor premise, foreign odors, like urine, and lost food can distract the interest of the dog.

- Placing the tins outside also can cause mixture of odors carried by the wind.

- By walking along the line of tins with the dog on a leash, the handler can influence the dog, either by his movement (walk slower, or stopping), by his voice, or by the leash. Handlers using dogs in scent identification line-ups have to be aware of the influences they can exert with their body language. The best way is for the dog to work off leash, letting the dog smell all the tins by himself at his own pace, and to keep still and not influence the dog in any way.

- If a correct match is made, and the tins are placed in another sequence with bare hands, all odors become contaminated, resulting in the dog's search work becoming highly dubious.

Uses in Criminal Cases

Although the basic principle has always been the same – match the odor of the corpus delicti to the odor of a suspect – the material used to present the odors, and the corresponding experimental protocol differs between countries. This has been a result of history and communication. A dog handlers' involvement in developing line-ups typically has been isolated to their own countries, and so differences have evolved. Only recently, information has been shared. The end of the Iron Curtain dividing West and Eastern Europe, and the closer integration of the European countries in the European Community, are both important factors in closing this gap.

A scent identification line-up can be used in criminal investigation by the police or as evidence in court. When used, they are limited by human rights and by local law. The general limits of Western Europe are to upholding the integrity of the human body, and that a person does not have to cooperate if it leads towards his own conviction. Collecting blood for scent identification line-ups would not be acceptable in Western European countries for this reason. However, suspects usually do have to cooperate and give their odor, be it from their hand or clothing. This is regulated by law. In the Netherlands, it is called a *measure in the interest of the investigation* and regarded similarly to taking a picture and a fingerprint.

As evidence in court trials, each country has its particular set of laws and regulations. This is closely linked to the very different cultural and law systems in these countries. In countries that have jury-based courts, there are usually strict limitations as to what can be presented as evidence and what cannot. The law of Frye is often followed. According to Frye, the following points need to be covered before a new type of research can be accepted in court as evidence:

- The method must be verifiable.
- Has it been tested, peer-reviewed and published.
- It must not have a known error rate.
- It must be standardized.
- It must be generally accepted.

Although these points are not completely followed for such generally accepted evidence as fingerprints or ballistics, new types of evidence are often scrutinized along these lines. Taslitz wrote a lengthy essay on this topic reviewing the status of scent line-ups, and titled them as 'unscientific myths'. In a recent book on the use of scientific evidence in judicial proceedings, the Polish scientist, Wójcikiewicz, also reviewed the status of scent identifications according to the

Hands of foils holding tubes: the preparation of material for a scent identification line-up in the Netherlands. (KLPD, 2002).

rule of Frye. He thinks that all of the points above have yet to be met, but notes that the method tends to be favorably perceived. If, in Europe, this direction continues, and more scientists get involved in research, it won't be long before the points of Frye can be met and the method can be presented as evidence in all countries that have adopted Frye.

International Standards

Dutch standard: Case with material for a scent identification line-up. (KLPD, 2002).

Countries with a long tradition of scent identification line-ups began by using them as a criminal investigation tool, often using a single dog for quick results and to link the crime to the suspect. This often led to a confession, which could then be presented in court. Gradually the method became more and more accepted and even mentioned as key motivations of the verdicts. This is typically the case in the Netherlands, where coupled with research, has led to significant improvements in the official methods and protocols – even though the procedures continue to draw such conflicting opinions.

In the United States, there is no such official standard, but supporters say scent identification line-ups are a powerful crime-fighting tool. It helps investigators to crack cases across the country. Critics of scent identification line-ups in the United States say, the problem is that dog handlers aren't certified or regulated, and that there isn't a system in place to check a dog's tracking record.

Again we quote Ed Lavandera, 'Steve Nicely is a professional dog trainer in Austin, Texas. He's trained police dogs for thirty years and is also an expert witness. He argues there needs to be a system in place that tracks a dog's accuracy rate. 'There are no national standards,' Nicely said. 'Our standards are so lacking, it's pathetic. We should be ashamed of ourselves.'

The Innocence Project of Texas (IPOT) wrote: 'Today, police and prosecutors are using yet another kind of junk science to win cases. This 'science' involves dog handlers who testify that a dog 'told' them who was present at a crime scene or whose scent was on a piece of evidence by making signals to the handler during a 'scent line-up'. The use of this 'dog whispering' has become more and more common. Prosecuters have touted the 'evidence' gained from this practice as being 'as powerful as DNA evidence to support a conviction. So, we decided to investigate the use of this technique by Texas officials.' And in their conclusions the IPOT wrote: 'The 'science' of scent line-ups in Texas has no rules, procedures or performance standards. It is being practiced by 'experts' without expertise according to no rules except their own.'

K9 Fraud!

Chapter 2:
Dogs' Responsiveness to Human Gestures

Everyone who has ever tried to teach a dog something knows that dogs respond very well to handler cues. Most people will also recognize that dogs pick up cues that they were not specifically trained for. For example, if you put on your walking shoes, the dog will stick to you like glue, because he expects to go for a walk. The question is how subtle can these cues be, and if dogs can pick up cues that, you yourself, are completely unconscious of. These kinds of cues are called the 'Clever Hans' effect, based on the apparent mathematic abilities of a horse named Hans.

Clever Hans Effect

CLEVER HANS WAS A STALLION, that lived at the turn of the twentieth century in Germany. He racked the brains of the animal psychologist of his time, and is still of importance in training dogs. The owner of this horse, Wilhelm von Osten, was an odd, eccentric person with a peculiarly eccentric idea. He believed that a horse was at least as intelligent as a human. He was absolutely convinced that a horse could count, read and think, and set out to prove his belief.

The first thing he did was give his horse, Hans, a language. After careful consideration for the way his horse could communicate,

The stallion 'Clever Hans' during one of his performances.

he chose tapping the horse's front hoof. All letters in the alphabet, and every number consisted of a specific number of taps of Hans' hoof. The training of this language came with a lot of difficulties. In the beginning, Wilhelm von Osten took Hans' hoof with his hands and taught him the language. This taught the horse how to communicate with his hoof without the help of Wilhelm, and after some time the animal seemed to understand this language.

On June 28, 1902, in a paper called 'Militärwochenblatt,' Wilhelm ran an advertisement with the following text: 'I want to sell my seven-year old, fine, docile stallion – which I do tests in order to determine the intellectual powers of horses. The horse distinguishes ten colors, reads, knows the four main processes of calculation, and a lot more. Von Osten, Griebenowstrasse 10, Berlin.'

'A lot more' referred to the horses ability to spell, distinguish notes of music, identify coins, play cards and tell the time. However, Von Osten did not want to sell Hans; by running the advertisement he only wanted to spark people's interest for his horse, and to share his opinion that animals are creatures with keen minds. To the annoyance of Wilhelm von Osten, nobody responded to his advertisement, as it was believed to be a late-April Fool's joke.

A Miraculous Horse

Only after a second advertisement did Von Osten get a response. This was his opportunity to show the capabilities of his horse. So, a select group of invited guests were allowed to question Hans – and the horse knew a lot of things. Hans could tell the date, what time it was, convert fractions into decimals, add, subtract, multiply and divide. The people who attended left awe-struck at Hans' amazing abilities.

The word of 'Kluger Hans' (Clever Hans) made it's way around in the country, and even gained international press coverage. A lot of people thought it was a scam, but the reports were so impressive that animal psychologist became enthusiastic and wanted to examine the horse more carefully. To the astonishment of everyone, Wilhelm von Osten had no intention to capitalize on his miraculous horse.

A committee of leading scientists researched the horse, and afterwards could not take a position on the horse's intelligence. One scientist admitted that Hans was no circus trick. This hesitation of the scientists, in examining Hans, shows how deceptive animals can be – such is the same with dogs. On August 11 1904, C.G. Schillings wrote in the 'Lokal-Anzeiger', a Berlin newspaper: 'I want to state outright, that the stallion understands the German language, numarical figures and artimatic at the level of a thirteen-year-old child. He distinguishes a lot of different colors, the correct names geometric figures, knows melodies and names, and reacts to questions just like as a human would . . .'

Subtle Movements

It was the animal psychologist, Oskar Pfungst, who exposed Clever Hans' secret of intelligence. Pfungst carefully observed the way the horse worked, and also watched mannerisms Von Osten. It was clear to him that this was not a trick, but believed that Hans' ability could be explained. Pfungst needed to be alone with the horse. When he was, he questioned the stallion and the animal answered in his typical fashion with his hoof. For a normal human without animal psychology training, there would be no doubt that the horse indeed could think and speak for itself; however, Pfungst had another experiment in mind. When in the company of others, he asked Hans questions of which nobody in the room knew the answer to, the results were surprising. The stallion started tapping his hoof and didn't stop – or as Pfungst wrote: 'The animal showed to be absent minded'. It was clear the stallion waited for a cue to stop tapping. This cue couldn't be given, because nobody present knew the answer to the question. The animal psychologist believed he had figured out the secret behind Hans' intelligence, and wrote: 'During the lengthy time it took to train Hans to communicate, the horse had learned to watch carefully for the small changes in posture from his teacher. These unconscious movements guided the result of Hans, where he used these cues as a sign to stop tapping. The motive for the horse to please the owner was apparent, as a reward for his attentiveness, he was regularly given carrots and bread. Through these means, Hans had acquired confident perception of the subtle movements of his owner; regardless, Hans is stunning.'

Clever Dog Nora

Wilhelm von Osten was unsuccessful in proving that mental capacity of a horse is parallel to human intellegence. But his four years of laborious training produced evidence that an animal takes cues from the slightest human movements; gestures that normally, even in human observation, are unseen.

Emilio Rendich, a painter, was another doubter of the abilities of Hans. He had also observed that Hans responded to Von Osten's mannerisms. He trained his dog, Nora, to respond in much the same way. The dog would respond to Rendich's questions, and when the correct was reached, Rendich would lean forward and Nora would stop. Unfortunately, Rendich's work is only described in a rather inaccessible and rare German book by K. Krall from 1912. However, Rendich showed that his dog was capable of using the same small physical cues.

Test with Signs

Dogs can learn to use such cues but learn them faster, as more recently proved by Hungarian scientist Dr. Ádám Miklósi in his study of the subject in 1998. He explored whether dogs used cues such as pointing, bowing, nodding, turning ones head, and glancing. In his experiment, the dog was positioned three meters in front of two pots, one of which contained food. The experimenter stood between the pots and gave the dog its cue, and then the dog could choose freely. After a number of these experiments, he tried the same test but with a different group of dogs. Their performance in the first fifteen trials was compared with the last fifteen trials.

The first group of dogs was one and a half years old, and in training to become disability assistant dogs. As a group, all six dogs could use pointing as a cue without training. Some of the dogs responded to bowing as a cue, but most were able to learn to use it during the training. Most dogs also learned nodding quite easily. Head turning was a lot more difficult to learn, and only three dogs managed to learn this. Only one of the dogs was able to learn glancing as a cue.

The second group of dogs was older than the first, and had lived with families

Chapter 2

Communication between the dog and man is based on a multitide of interactions. A dog naturally learns these cues.

for a long time. These dogs had not received explicit training throughout their life. They were trained on the same gestures and in the same manner as above. All dogs responded to pointing, bowing, and nodding without training in the first fifteen trials. Three dogs responded immediately to head turning. The others learned to respond, and their performance increased during the trials. The dogs could not use glancing as a cue without training, but four out of the six dogs learned to use this cue during the experiment. This second group was subsequently tested with another experimenter to see if the cues were independent from the person giving them.

The conclusion was that the dogs naturally take the cues of their owners. Dr. Miklósi argues that the dogs are not simply forming an association between a cue and the place of a reward, but that there is actual communication between the dog and handler based on these interactions, and that the dogs understand the meaning of these cues.

Glancing Cues

By minor body movements, encourages and slight influences at the tracking line, the dog handler leads his dog intentional or unintentional over the track.

In 2001, Dr. Krisztina Soproni and her colleagues experimented more extensively on eye contact cues. A comparison was made between the different types of eye contact – looking at a dog directly with both eyes and head, facing the dog with the head, but no eye contact, and keeping the head still while making eye contact. The dogs had been trained to use pointing as a key signal, so, a number of trials with these other three cues became a part of the pointing training.

Each cue was presented eight times to fourteen dogs. The dogs responded significantly to direct head and eye contact, but randomly to the head only or eyes only contact. Next, the responses during the first four sessions were compared with the last four sessions. There was no difference in the direct head and eyes cue or the head only cue. The eyes only cue was avoided during the first sessions, and used move extensively during the last sessions. It was argued that the dogs, in the beginning, might misinterpret the eyes-only cue, since prolonged eye contact within Canid communication is used by dominant individuals. However, the dogs learned its correct meaning quickly, even though they received this cue less than the other two eye cues. This stresses the importance of eyes as a method of communication.

Pointing Gestures

In 2002, the same Hungarian scientist, Dr. Krisztina Soproni and her colleagues, tested the dog's responsiveness to physical pointing gestures. In the test, the dogs could find food pellets at a place where the experimenter was pointing. Six male and three female dogs between the ages of two to seven years old took part in the test. Except for three of the dogs, all of them had lived with human families since they were puppies; the other three joined a family as an adult. Four of the dogs had taken part in Dr. Soproni's experiments a year earlier, but, were considered naïve with respect to the current experiment at hand. The observations were carried out in the owners' apartments. Only the experimenter – Dr. Krisztina Soproni, the owner, and the dog were present during the training and testing. Two brown plastic flowerpots, both fifteen centimeters in diameter and height, were used to hide the food. Both pots had double bottoms where one food pellet was fixed. This was done to confuse the dog's sense of smell. The bottom panels were covered with a piece of cloth to prevent any noise from occurring during the baiting. Various brands of dry food were experimented with and used as reward.

In the pre-training, the experimenter stood half a meter behind the two flower pots, which were one meter apart and on chairs. The owner restrained the dog two meters in front of the pots. The experimenter tried to make eye contact

A: The experimental setting. B: Pointing and far-pointing. C: Reverse pointing. D: Stick pointing. E: Reverse stick pointing. F: Elbow cross-pointing and far elbow cross-pointing. G: Elbow pointing. H: Long cross-pointing. I: Short cross-pointing.

Different pointing gestures used in the experiments of Soproni and her collegues, in 2002.

and called the dog by its name. When the dog was attentive to the gestures of the experimenter, she showed the dog a food pellet and placed it into one of the containers. Then the owner allowed the dog to approach the pots and choose one of them. If the dog chose the baited pot, then it could eat the reward and was also praised verbally by the owner. If the dog made the incorrect choice and went to the empty pot, then the experimenter took the pellet from the other pot and showed it to the dog. In this case, the dog didn't get the food. This trial was repeated four times; the position of the food was changed every time. The pre-training was necessary to ensure that the dogs knew that the flower pots might contain food.

During the testing the position of the subjects was the same, but now the dog was prevented from observing which pot the food was placed. After the food was hidden, the owner stood behind the dog and made it sit facing the experimenter. The owner was asked to let the dog go after the experimenter had given the cue. The experimenter made eye contact with the dog and indicated the location of the food with a various types of pointing gestures.

In a series of three experiments, dogs were presented with variations of pointing gestures; gestures with reversed direction of movement, cross-pointing, and different arm extensions. Dogs performed at a respectable level if they could see the index finger of the experimenter. If that was not available to them, dogs still could rely on the body position of the signaler. The direction of movement of the arm did not influence the performance. In summary, these observations suggest that dogs are able to rely on relatively common gestural forms of human movement and that they are able to comprehend, to some extent, the referential nature of human pointing.

The Detour Test

Dr. Péter Pongrácz and his colleagues from the department of Ethology in the University of Budapest examined social learning of dogs, namely, the effect of human gestures on the performance of dogs in taking detours to perform a task. They recorded the behavior of dogs in these detour tests, in which an object, such as a favorite toy or food, was placed behind a V-shaped fence. Dogs were able to master this task; however, they did it more easily when they started from within the fence with the object placed outside. Repeated detours, starting from within the fence, did not help the dogs to obtain the object more quickly if in a subsequent trial the dog and object were reversed. While six trials were not enough for the dogs to show significant improvement on their own, demonstration of this action by humans significantly improved the dog's performance within two to three trials. Owners and strangers were equally effective as demonstrators. Their experiments show that dogs are able to rely on information provided by human action when confronted with a new task. While they didn't copy the exact path of the human demonstrator, they easily adopted the detour behavior shown by humans to reach their goal.

K9 Fraud!

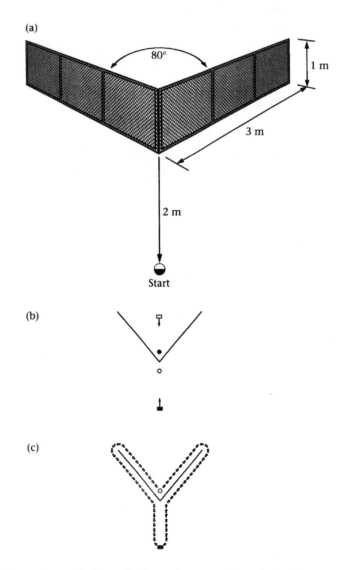

Drawing of the V-shaped experimental fence in the experiments of Pongrácz and his collegues in 2001.

(a): The steel-framed wire-mesh fence was fixed into the soil by its protruding pegs. The starting point for the Inward Detour group is indicated. (b): Sketch from above of the position of the starting point (black and white square) and the position of the target (black and white circle). Black is the Inward Detour group; white is the Outward Detour group. (c): A sketch from above of a possible demonstration route; the other demonstration route is the reverse of the one presented. The human demonstrator carried the object to the inside intersection angle of the fence (black arrows) put it down and left the fence (white arrows).

Chapter 2

Working 'Blind'

The importance of all these experiments is that they illustrate how well dogs can learn to 'read' us. The case of Clever Hans demonstrates the extent to which an animal is able to observe and to respond to subtle human gestures. But since the famous story of Hans, a lot of this knowledge has been lost, even to professionals. This results to a lot of faults in training as well as in practice.

It is widely believed that the success of dogs in becoming 'man's best friend' was due to their ability to adapt to several aspects of human behavior and social organization. Since humans continuously and unconsciously use gestures in their communicative interactions, dogs are highly responsive to these cues.

As we could see from all the tests before, dogs are very sensitive to human gestural communication. Dogs are able to utilize pointing, bowing, nodding, head-turning and glancing gestures as cues for finding hidden objects. Dogs are also able to generalize from one person, to another in using the same gestures as cues.

During training, we want the dogs to respond to the relevant cue. So, when searching for an odor, the only cue must be the odor. When observing handlers with their dogs, sometimes a handler's physical cues are too obvious. In scent identification line-ups, dogs can be seen hovering over each odor in the line, carefully watching their handler. The slightest movement is enough for them to respond to that odor based on the physical cues. Also in police detector dogs this can be seen, for instance, as soon as the dog enters the hiding place and the handler makes a small step forward, the dog will respond to such cues. But how can we prevent ourselves from cueing the dog in some way, if they can pick up and use such minimal cues? The answer is obvious: work 'blind.' Do not know the position of the matching odor or the hiding place, and preferably have no one close by who knows it since this person may also unconsciously cue the dog. Such measures will enormously increase the independent performance of the dog.

K9 Fraud!

In order to avoid the handler's influence, do not know the position of the matching odor - or the hiding place, and preferably have no one close by who knows it since this person may also unconsciously cue the dog.

Chapter 3:
Fraud with Tracking Dogs

Late 2008, William Dillon was relieved when he left Florida's toughest prison after having been incarcerated for twenty seven years – innocent in jail for a murder that he was later exonerated for. DNA evidence excluded him from being connected to a key piece of evidence. By that it also became clear that the 'evidence' John Preston and his German Shepherd Dog, 'Harras II,' produced was fraudulent...

JOHN PRESTON, a former Pennsylvania Highway Patrol Trooper, had followed with his dog an eight days old track over Highway 1A through the busy town of Titusville in Florida that ended in the house of William Dillon. Preston and his dog, Harass II, conducted two tests which he said linked the T-shirt to the crime scene and Dillon to the T-shirt. In the second test, a 'paper lineup,' which allegedly linked Dillon to the T-shirt. Preston allowed his dog to sniff the T-shirt and then pieces of paper, including one Dillon had touched. Preston said the dog selected Dillon's paper, and Dillon was arrested and charged with the murder. After a five-day trial, William Dillon was convicted of first-degree murder at James Dvorak in August 1981 and sentenced to life in prison.

Unfortunately Dillon was not the only one who by the frauded 'evidence' of Preston was sent to prison. Preston put at least fifteen men behind bars and, in some cases, on Death Row. Among them:

Gary Bennett, sentenced to life in prison for the 1983 murder of a woman neighbor in Palm Bay.

Frank Berry, sentenced to 124 years in prison for raping a Merritt Island woman in 1981.

Scott Carroll, a serial rapist suspected in numerous Brevard County cases, tried and convicted in New York where he remains in prison.

Wilton Dedge, exonerated and released in 2004 after spending twenty two years in prison for a 1981 rape that DNA evidence showed he didn't commit.

Gary Dirk, sentenced to life in prison for burglary and rape in 1985.

James Elmen, seventeen years old when a jury acquitted him of burglary and murder charges in 1984.

Mark Wayne Jones, serving double life sentences for the murders of two Titusville women to whom he had given a ride in 1981.

Elton Kimbrough and *Kenneth Michael Burch*, murder charges dropped, sentenced to ten years on burglary charges, in the robbery and death of an eighty nine-year-old Titusville woman.

Juan Ramos, found not guilty during a second trial in 1987 after being sentenced to death for rape and murder of a neighbor in 1982.

Willie Jessie Snipes, paroled in 1986 after serving four years for manslaughter that occurred during a robbery in 1981.

Gerald Stano, a serial killer who confessed to forty one murders. He was convicted in Brevard County for the murder of seventeen-year-old Cathy Lee Scharf in 1983 and executed.

Christopher Wilder, a serial killer who was killed during a struggle with Massachusetts police in 1984. He was accused of murdering a Satellite Beach resident earlier that year.

Eugene Wiley, served eleven years for second-degree murder in the death of a Saudi Arabian exchange student in an alleged drug deal.

In all states of America where Preston appeared with his magic dog, he claimed to perform tracking feats that frankly, aren't even physically possible for a tracking dog, no matter how well-trained, or how good that dog is. And Preston's dogs weren't well-trained. He travelled around the country, dropping in to work with police, then testify about his dog's 'finds,' first having been court certified as an expert. The only problem: he wasn't an expert, and neither his tracking evidence nor his testimony was reliable.

Chapter 3

Historical Tracking Dogs

From the time of Plinius, a mosaic floor at the enterance of an old Roman house in Pompeï. (AD 79) with the well-known warning 'Cave Canem'
(Beware of the Dog.)

The police dog in the protection service probably goes back a long way. As long as we have documented history the dog has been companion and guardian to the men protecting the peace. First as faithful comrade of the old-time night watchman with his horn and his halberd, gradually evolving into our present-day police dog in the surveillance police and intelligence services.

We can find traces of tracking dogs in the service of forensic investigation quite a long way back in history, the oldest being found among the ancient Greeks. An ancient papyrus found in Egypt contained a satire by Sophocles (496-406 B.C.) called 'Ichneutai' ('The Tracking Dogs'.) This somewhat risqué burlesque describes the theft, well known in mythology, of the herds of Apollo by Hermes. Sophocles describes how satyrs, masquerading as herding dogs, pursue the track of the stolen herd and the robber. This illustrates that the Greeks at the time of Sophocles were well acquainted with the use of dogs for such tracking work.

In the time of the Roman empire, Plinius (A.D. 23-79) described in his 'Naturalis Historia' six categories of dogs: villatici (home – or guard dogs,) pastorales pecuarii (shepherd dogs,) venatici (hunting dogs,) pugnaces and bellicosi (fight or wardogs,) pedibus celeres (sighthounds) and nares sagaces (tracker dogs.)

Much later in the late Middle Ages, a book in translation titled 'Book of hawks, goshawks, sparrow-hawks, horses, and dogs' by Heinrich Mynsinger was published (1473.) The author based his book on much older sources and speaks of regular police dog training which involved training the dog to stand up against a man clothed 'in a stout coat of skins lest the dog should bite him during his education.' The dogs were also trained to track the trail of a thief, much in the same way that bird dogs (retrievers) are taught to search for partridge and quail. Mynsinger describes how a Doctor Meurer wrote about the tracking work of dogs and their training in 1460, basing his views on English standards. Later again, Capt. Max von Stephanitz refers to the painter W. von Kuegelgen of Dresden in a book he wrote in 1923. This painter wrote memoirs called 'Youthful reminiscences of an old man,' where he tells us how police dogs had been used to search for his father who had been murdered near the town. Finally, let us mention what M. Siber tells us in his book published in 1899. He relates how the Kaffirs used the native dogs to track the 'spoor' of men and that, according to E. von Weber, 'they often go out and bring back their runaway lady-loves with the help of dogs.'

Woodcut from Mynsinger (1473): The dogs were also trained to track the trail of a thief.

In his book published in 1923, Capt. Max von Stephanitz wrote:

'I wish to emphasize that it was the shepherd dog who inaugurated the police dog movement, and that it is he who is the moving spirit in it today. Our shepherd dog is a born police dog, for when he is with the flocks and the herds he is also a 'policeman.' He maintains law and order, looks after the safety of his charges, punishes delinquents and turns back trespassers. His development in the past from the dog of the Bronze Age to Hovawart, sheep and cattle dog, fostered and strengthened those very characteristics and inclinations which would make him the police dog per excellence: i.e. joy in work, devotion to duty, loyalty to his master, mistrust and sharp awareness of strangers and unusual things, docility and obedience, teachability and quickness to understand, as well as immunity to weather, uncommonly acute senses, and an uncanny gift for retrieving and seeking.'

Night Watchmen

The Belgian author Louis Huyghebaert wrote about the general view that the shepherd dog was trusted from the beginning for the role of police dog in a series published in 1925: 'It is not easy to determine the precise time the dog started work in this role. An old document illustrating a dog in this role is an early 17th century woodcut. This woodcut shows a night watchman on duty in the Belgian town of Antwerp accompanied by a dog. The city archives mention that the first night watchman in Antwerp was chartered in 1597, and by 1627 there were thirty two men on duty.' It is conceivable that protection dogs accompanied these men. Looking at the woodcut these earlier police dogs were apt to bite as much as they are nowadays: we see the dog at the first command helping his master by boldly biting the legs of the villain! The weapons of the night watchmen seen in the front of the woodcut show us that they performed a serious task. The halberd and the long saber were used to bring a villain to the lockup and in the background his colleagues can be seen doing just that. Together with these weapons the night watchmen made increasing use of their police dogs, as can be seen in a print with 'New Year's greetings of the night watchmen from the Belgian town of Leuven' in the year 1786.

K9 Fraud!

Night watchman of the Belgian town Antwerp accompanied by a police dog. Woodcut from the early 17th century.

Chapter 3

New Year's greetings from the night watchmen from the Belgian town of Leuven. Woodcut from 1786.

K9 Fraud!

Police Tracking Dogs

Demonstration of a police dog in Belgium, 1899

After the French Revolution 1793 the use of police dogs in Belgium was abolished. The 'Human Rights' manifesto declared by the new regime contained a ban on dogs attacking people. But this new declaration may have been prompted by the fact that the police dogs had become too sharp and agressive for public acceptance. After the abolition of the police dogs in Belgium, more than a century passed before public administration resumed the use of dogs in police service.

About 1890 dog enthusiasts around the Belgian city Malines started to systematically train their Malinois, the shorthaired Belgian shepherd dog, for protection and tracking work. Louis Huyghebaert in particular encouraged the training of the dogs in nose work. In an article from that time we read: 'While we walked together along the canal, Mr. Huyghebaert gave me his wallet and during a moment when his dog 'Tom' was not watching, I threw the wallet in the brushwood about three meters from the road. After walking on for a longer distance, Tom's master began to search his pockets and gesticulated as if he lost something. Immediately the dog went back to the place where we had briefly paused and came back without having found anything. Seeing his master still inspecting his pockets, he ran back faster, first tracking and then searching with his nose in the air. Soon he came back with a triumphant look in his eyes and the wallet in his mouth.'

It was in the Belgian town of Gent that Superintendent Van Wezemael brought about the introduction of three police dogs in March 1899. At the end of the same year there were already ten dogs, and 1910 more than thirty! All these dogs were Belgian shepherd dogs, and most of them were of the Groenendael and Malinois variety. They were not only trained for protection work but also for nose work.

Dog-Detectives

The use of these police dogs was such a success that soon many other Belgian towns, and even countries abroad, followed this example. Numerous newspaper articles (especially English and French) full of praise caused such a demand for shepherds, that all the look-alikes of Groenendael, the black longhaired Belgian shepherd dog, and Malinois were exported to England, France, Germany, Russia, Argentina and the United States. In most of these countries (police) dog-training societies were founded.

Right from the introduction, police dogs captured the interest of journalists and the general public in these different countries. This increased significantly when the dogs began to work as 'detectives' investigating criminal cases. The value of the police dog was fully recognized when the first successes in solving homicides were recorded; from that moment on the dogs became very popular. These first criminal investigations by dogs caused quite a stir all over the world. The police dog movement, at that time still in its infancy, profited substantially.

A German policeman with his dog about 1910

It is interesting to read the German reports of that time, which contain unbelievable (or incredible) tracking results. In a number of cases the dogs also perform suspect identification in scent line-ups after following the track. An anthology is given below; these examples were taken from Schmidt's book on police dog successes he published in 1911. In a lot of these stories the presumption of foreknowledge about the suspect and clear fraud occurres:

- 'In 1910 police dog 'Bolko' of the Berlin police worked out a seven days old track and marked not only the place where the body of a murdered teacher was found near the river, but also tracked for two hours to a pub in the next village where he barked to a chair the teacher had been sitting on. Based on this a man who was seen with the teacher in the pub was arrested. The teacher should in a few days make a statement in court against the suspect.'

- April 4 1910 police dog 'Harras I' of the Cottbus' police worked out a two days old track after getting odor from a matchbox found near the place of a fire. He followed the about 800 metres long track of an 11-years old boy who caused the fire.'

- 'An 18 hours old and 3 kilometres long track of an arsonist was worked out with strong sidewind by police dog 'Wolf v.d. Treue' in 1910 and led to the house of the suspect.'

- 'In Flehingen near Bretten during the night of October 20 to 21 1906 a burglary took place in a post office by which a person was serious injured. The next day a suspect was arrested, but denied. At October 24 the German Shepherd Dog 'Luchs v. Frankfurt' was brought at the crime scene. There the dog was given time to take in the oder of the crime scene and a pair of socks of the suspect that were brought in. After that the dog tracked with his nose deep to the ground surface, first around the village and after that on the railway dam to the village of Bretten. Shortly before Bretten the dog lost the track, but found it back immediately after the village on the road to Dühren-Enzberg, and worked out the track untill Enzberg. The distances are: Flehingen-Bretten-Mühlacker-Enzberg = 28 kilometres including sometimes walking back of the dog on the track. In Enzberg, the residence of the suspect, was stayed over, and next day Luchs tracked in one line to the suspect's house. After the door was opened the dog walked up the stairs to an attic room. There stood between two cupboards a bag the dog barked to and tried to retrieve it. After some time the wife in the house admitted that the bag belonged to the suspect. In the bag nothing suspicious was found. After being confronted with the work of the dog the suspect submitted to have been in the post office, but denied to be the burglar.

Finding the knife by which he injured the person failed. On the long way the suspect had enough time to dispose of it in a way it is also for the dog's nose untraceable. Would Luchs have been tracked the next days, and not after four days it for sure would have been possible for him to find also this piece of evidence.'

Other Miraculous Stories

The police dog literature of these early years often mentions similar miraculous stories. Most of the trainers, together with the journalist writing the accounts, speak in exaggerated terms about the results of these dogs. Within the police and in judicial circles the work of the police dogs was fully trusted, and the clues provided by the dogs were accepted as solid evidence. Based on what we know today, these results were often influenced by the handler or the 'most likely' suspect.

- 'To clear up a murder case, Inspector Bussenius from Braunschweig was called in 1908 to the city of Mannheim with both his dogs, 'Harras' and 'Max'. The dogs unanimously picked out Becker a furniture maker, a number of times out of a group of people. Becker was already suspected of this murder, and soon after he admitted his guilt.'
- 'On December 24th, 1908, a sex murder of a ten year old boy took place in the woods surrounding the town of Giessen. In spite of his denial, the suspected cobbler apprentice Reif was arrested. To establish conclusive proof of the suspect's guilt, the police dog 'Greif von Wetzlar' together with his handler Police-sergeant Jacob, tried to follow the track on the 27th of December in the afternoon. Greif was given the clothes from the child to pick up scent. The murderer undoubtedly handled these clothes. The dog searched from the crime scene along a 3.5 km long track even though at least 72 hours had elapsed since the murder. To make matters worse, the ground was frozen stiff and a biting wind was blowing. Further work had to be stopped due to the onset of darkness. The next day the public prosecutor ordered several groups of persons to be placed along the track established the previous day. Among them was the suspect Reif. After Greif was once again presented the clothes, he picked up on the same track, until

Succesful tracking to the house of the suspect.

And even a boot of the suspect was found as evidence.

he came to the line up of people. The dog sniffed briefly at first two persons, but when he came to the third person, the suspect Reif, he sniffed him, barked then lunged at Reif's chest so violently that they could hardly bring Greif away from Reif. After some time Reif confessed to the murder.'

- 'In October 1909, Police-sergeant Jacob and 'Greif von Wetzlar' solved another homicide case by picking up a trail, which was several days old, through the whole town right into a room on the first floor of a restaurant/inn.'

- 'On Sunday October 17 1909, the forester Firnkes was stabbed and killed in a field near the village of Bruchsal; his body was found on Monday. Before the police arrived, the body and the crime scene had been looked over by many inquisitive people and all evidential traces and tracks were destroyed. On the evening of the 19th the prosecutor contacted the police dog unit in the nearby town of Weinheim and requested them to come to the crime scene. So, on the 20th of October, three police dogs from the town Weinheim arrived in Bruchsal. That morning, gendarmes had arrested a person called Feuerstein. Feuerstein was known as a poacher and he was suspected because he had been seen coming out of the fields that Sunday. Of course Feuerstein denied everything. He was told to put on the clothes that he had worn on that Sunday. Subsequently he was lined up between 15 other persons fifty steps away from where the body still lay. The police dogs, all German Shepherd Dogs, were separated. First a male, 'Melac' was brought to smell the body still lying at the crime scene. He was then led to the lined up persons. Soon after that Melac began to bark at Feuerstein, upon whose trousers stains were found that could have been washed out blood. The police dog 'Pia' also barked at Feuerstein when put through the same routine. The test had to be stopped here, because the body had to be brought to the town hall for autopsy. In the yard of the town hall 'Irma von Flügelrade' sniffed the clothes of the murdered forester. Feuerstein was again placed in line between other persons and Irma also barked at him. He was arrested after that on suspicion of murder, and after short time he confessed.'

- 'Near the town of Westpriegnitz at the Dallmin estate, which belonged to the former Minister of Agriculture his Excellency Otto von Podbielski, a nine year old girl was lured from the street into a pine forest and killed on the morning of November 20 1909. In the evening the child was found. The next day two policemen with their German Shepherd Dogs 'Prinz v. Mühlenberg' and 'Bolko v. Klostermansfeld' went to Dallmin. In the meantime an attempt to pick up a track had already been tried with a Airedale Terrier police dog from Havelberg and the servants of the manor had carried out a search. All without result. At the crime scene, where the body still lay, Prinz picked up the odor of the clothes of the child. Due to the onset of darkness his handler worked with him on a long leash. It snowed continuously. Prinz first tracked through the woods then in the direction of the estate coach-house. When they reached this house the track couldn't be followed anymore because of the deep snow. The search for the murderer then concentrated on the persons at the estate. One of them, a laborer with scratches in his face, was taken into custody. The gardener's helper Pöhling was also suspected, although he was thought to be innocent by the father of the murdered child as well as the examining magistrate. Both suspects stubbornly denied their involvement. Pöhling was placed in line between other servants of the estate. Prinz sniffed at the pinafore of the child, since in the opinion of his handler this was the place with the strongest odor of the perpetrator, considering it was a sexually motivated murder. After that the dog searched around in the room, coming up to the line and smelling a number of them without making a sign. But after sniffing Pöchling he immediately started barking, and while barking he clearly made a signal by looking alternatively at his handler and at Pöhling. Suddenly as if Prinz feared his signal could be misunderstood, he bit Pöhling in his leg. Pöhling again protested his innocence and explained that the dog only came to him because during the search for the lost child he had taken the body under the arm and lifted it up. Pöhling was told the dog had only sniffed at the lower part of the pinafore, which meant that he, Pöhling, must have also touched that area. After that, Pöhling made a detailed confession, and also told he stabbed the child in the neck with a pocketknife that he had thrown in a nearby thicket. Pöhling also recounted that he had read a lot about police dogs and thought he was protecting himself by making his way back in a loop through the water and over a wire fence, hoping to erase his track in this way. The next day, the 22nd of November, the other dog, 'Bolko' took the scent from the hands of the murderer in the vicinity of the crime scene and after a short time discovered the knife used for the crime under a pine tree.'

- 'In the German town Münden during the night of February 1 1910, several windowpanes in the house of an industrialist were broken. Twelve hours later Police Sergeant Hattenbach from Hannover arrived with his German Shepherd Dog 'Afra v. Gahrenberg'. Afra picked up the scent from one of the stones that was thrown into the room. She searched for the scent of the perpetrator, leading the team over 200 meters to a workman's house, where she barked at the door of a man named Sievert. The man was not home but at work in a leather factory. Sergeant Hattenbach went there with 'Afra'. He gave her the scent of the stone once again and sent her to search. There were 36 workers in the factory. 'Afra' sniffed every man and in spite of the acrid odor of tan, leather, etc. she soon was barking at Sievert. And even though the man denied it, he later paid for the window panes voluntary.'

- 'On Monday the 9th of January 1911 a thief crept into the estate of a brewery owner called Dirigl in the German town of Vilsiburg. He was caught by a stable boy while putting oats into a sack, but escaped leaving the sack and one carpet slipper. The stable boy was not sure he had recognized the thief but assumed the thief was Dionys Riemer. On Monday January 23, a fortnight later, the police dog 'Varus v. Altfeld' and his handler were ordered to go to Vilsiburg in order to find out if the lost slipper belonged to the suspected Mr. Riemer or not. Because Riemer was not home, a jacket that belonged to him was laid down behind his house, and the dog picked up the scent from the slipper in front of the house. The dog barked at the jacket and also at a broom lying in a barn. Inquiry revealed that Mr. Riemer had brought this broom home shortly before. When Riemer returned home the dog immediately attacked him. Hereupon the suspect was placed among other persons and 'Varus' again picked up the scent from the slipper. Each time he attacked Riemer, who was sentenced to three months in prison on the basis of the full conviction of the dog and other circumstantial evidence on February 7, in spite of continued stubborn denial.'

- 'For years a court secretary in the town of Dieuze was pestered by the worst type of anonymous letters. After hearing of the incredible results of the police dogs he consulted Frontier Inspector Obst, who advised him to get property of the persons that could be connected to the letters. These objects were hidden in various places. Inspector Obst let his German Shepherd Dog 'Roland v. Martinsberg' pick up scent from the last of the anonymous letters. This nine-day-old letter had been sent to the Department in Strassburg. From there it was brought to the court in Dieuze and handed over to the victimized secretary, so it had passed through several hands. After Roland picked up the scent of this letter he was sent to search. During several searches he always fetched property belonging to a Mrs. Zimmerman. The dog was allowed to sniff Mrs. Zimmerman's hat then he was brought the hidden letter. Although the suspect denied, the court convicted her. After this success, Inspector Obst received many requests for help in similar cases, particularly from France.'

Bold Dog Handlers

From October 1909, the SV, the 'Verein für deutsche Schäferhunde' ('German Shepherd Dog Society'), offered a 25 Mark reward to the dog handler for every homicide case successfully solved by a German Shepherd Dog. In a period of eighteen months the SV paid this cash prize 18 times!

Friedo Schmidt wrote about this in his 1911 book that contains hundreds of success stories with police dogs of that time: 'In this way, rapidly one case after the other was solved, so that we can now look back upon a considerable number of murder cases successfully settled by the work of German Shepherd Dogs. This success cannot only be attributed to the perfect aptitude of the dogs, but certainly also to our bold dog handlers.'

And by that 'bold dog handlers' he was right because a lot of cases from that time verges on the impossibility or even were imposible. For sure now we can say that a lot of these cases were *incorrect human interpretations*, *putting pressure on the 'most likely' suspect* with barking or biting dogs and/or *influencing of dogs by the handler*. Let's take a closer look at these three subjects.

Incorrect Human Interpretations

An event, described by J. Hansmann in 1931, shows the work of a tracking dog, and illustrates how a typical incorrect human interpretation of that work could be made if the dog wasn't brought back at the crime scene to work out a second suspicious spot:

'After a burglary indistinct footprints were found in the vicinity of the house, at two different places about one hundred meters distance from each other. A police dog handler from Berlin started with his dog at one of these spots. The dog picked up a track leading to the railway station. There it is said that an unknown suspiciously behaving man with a backpack, who could be described exactly, travelled from this small station with the first morning train to Berlin…

But the dog handler went back to the crime scene and brought his dog to the second place where indistinct footprints were found. The dog now followed a track three kilometers in another direction to a secluded garden house. In the garden, the dog stopped at a spot which had been recently dug up. Here the greater part of the spoil was found.'

This example certainly demonstrates the value of having a good police dog working in crime investigation but it also shows us how easily we can make mistakes in the explanation of the dog's work. If the dog handler had stopped after the track leading to the railway, the interpretation would have been that the man described with the backpack was carrying the stolen material away. This would not have led to a proper conclusion of the case at all.

Putting Pressure on the Suspect

A good example of putting pressure on the 'most likely' suspect with barking or biting dogs we read in the memoirs of Amsterdam Police Officer Jacob Water in the time about the First World War: 'The Public Prosecutor in Maastricht, a town in the south of the Netherlands, asked for assistance with my police tracking dog 'Albert'. In a settlement near the Belgian border three days before a murdered woman was found and the only corpus delicti found at the crime scene was a handkerchief. After walking several kilometres Albert leaded us to a cottage at a small path in the woods. The door was opened by a woman

After walking several kilometres, Albert led us to a cottage through a small path in the woods.

and Albert darted inside. Soon I heard him barking and found him standing on a bed. I saw someone hiding under the blankets, called Albert to me and soon the head of a man appeared. I proclaimed to be a policeman and order him to put on his clothes and to follow me.

Driving back to Maastricht the prosecuter started questioning, but the arrested man claimed to know nothing about it and to be innocent. 'Are you sure we got the right man?' the prosecuter whispered in my ear. But I whispered back to him: 'You will hear it out of his own mouth'. Thereupon I said to the man: 'Well, if you really are innocent, I'll tell the dog he is wrong. But be sure you can't deceive this dog. If you are lying I can't answer for the consequences'. By this I speculated on the fact that in the eyes of a criminal a police dog has something mysterious... and on a trick I learned Albert: to attack after I gave him a certain sign. So I said to the dog: 'Albert, boy, it seems you were wrong...' and gave him that sign. Growling he shoot to the man, who startled cried: 'Keep away that dog, yes I did it, I will confess!' And so this murder case was unofficial solved before we were back in Maastricht.'

And also in another case Officer Water wrote in his memoirs how his dog forced suspects to confess: 'That morning I went with Albert to the court. There I was told that two arrested men were suspect of a burglary, but denied. At the crime scene two caps were found that probably belonged to these men, although they negated. In this case Albert had to bring clearness. On my demand at the courtyard a circle was formed of policemen and other employees, and between them both suspects were standing about four metres from each other. I let Albert take scent from one of the caps, and after having sniffed some other persons, he stood barking in front of one of the suspects. After that Albert took scent of the second cap, passed over the first suspect and went to the second one. Both arrested men insist on their innocence. 'The dog propably made a mistake,' they said. 'Well,' I said, 'in that case I will tell him he was wrong.' Just like the other time in the car, my tricked hold true. Albert started growling and showed his teeth, after which the suspects suddenly reminded everything. They blamed each other, as usual, but they were put safe behind bars.'

Chapter 3

Influencing by the handler

As you could already read in the chapters before, dogs can quick react at even the smallest signs we often unconsciously give them. In psychology this effect is called 'Clever Hans' from a German horse that learned to count and calculate by pawing. The horse 'Hans' reacted on a small unconsciously given forward movement of the head of his master if he reached the correct answer, and used it as a sign to stop pawing.

Another way of influencing the dog is by the tracking leash wich forms the contact with the dog. Movements or pulling the leash is immediately noticeable by the dog. Working with the leash of course depends on the temperament and the burden capability of the dog. With a dynamic tension on the tracking leash we are able to control the speed of the dog and eventually increase his willingness to work. By increasing the tension on the leash we can stimulate a dog in difficult situations to go on. But a dog who is already pulling the leash will with a too taut leash even pull faster. These dogs most of the time need voice correction in order to obey, then even with a too low tension on the leash they will go much too fast. Also for a somewhat unsure dog who tracks slowly the tracking leash shouldn't be too taut, because such a dog can feel that as a correction. By too much pulling the leash and not keeping the leash at a correct tension the dog will get out of his concentration on the track by which he will make mistakes because of inattention and careless work.

A big mistake, often made on purpose, is act on the dog with the tracking leash, as for instance in training happens when the dog enters an article at the track or a turn. In such a case before entering the article or turn the sagging leash will be pulled tight, or the dog with a taut leash will be pulled back. After some time the dog will connect this pull tight or pull back with an article or a turn. He will not search anymore, but do as if he is tracking with his head to the ground, waiting for a sign of the handler. In this way a dog handler can lead his dog to a certain point he wants the dog to go.

Although in the time before the First World War, especially in Germany, a lot was written about 'Clever Hans' and the influence of human at animals most of the police dog handlers of that time omitted the results of this influencing.

Police and justice fully trusted the work of the police tracking dogs and their results were fully accepted as evidence in court.

Many Excesses

The possibilities of the police dogs in crime investigation were highly overestimated and this led to many excesses. The open criticism of the work of police dogs also produced priceless parodies, such as 'Remarkable Nose of a Police Dog' written by M. Soschtschenko in 1929: 'The fur coat belonging to Jeremje Bakkin, a merchant, was stolen. He was furious, because it was a very special fur. 'That fur,' he said, 'was a peach. The money doesn't matter, but we have to find the thief and punish him,' and he summoned a police dog to the scene. Soon a small man with a cap appeared in the village, accompanied by a medium-sized dog. It was a real cur, brown, with a pointed snout and an unpleasant expression. When he got near to the door the man put his dog on the thief's track, said 'psst', and let him go. The dog sniffed at the track and then looked at the spectators, local residents who had gathered to enjoy the spectacle. Suddenly the dog went to Grandma Fiokla who lived at number 5 and sniffed at her skirt. Grandma tried to hide herself behind the others but the dog grasped her skirt. Suddenly she fell on her knees in front of the police officer. 'Yes,' she said, 'I've been picked out and I don't deny it. I stole five buckets full of corn and a spirit lamp. Everything is in the bathroom. Take me to the police station.' At that all became silent. 'And the fur?', they asked. 'I know nothing of a fur,' she answered. 'But everything else is the truth, take me to the station and punish me.' Grandma was taken away.

The man put his dog back on the trail, said 'psst' and let him go. The animal again looked round and walked up to neighbor Upradow, who turned pale, fell on his knees and said: 'Yes, it's true. Slap the cuffs on me. I collected the waterworks money and did not hand it over, but spent it for personal use.' No wonder that he was immediately captured by the local residents and taken away.

Meanwhile the cur went to the resident of house number 7 and grasped his trousers. The neighbor's face blanched with fear and he fell on his knees. 'I'm guilty,' he exclaimed. 'I tampered with my year of birth; otherwise I would have had to go to war. Instead I had an easy life and I took advantage of it.' Those present got excited and wondered what kind of a special dog this was. Merchant Jeremje Bakkin blinked, took some money out of his pocket and handed it to the policeman and said: 'Take your dog away. For all I care that fur will never be found. Go to hell with your dog.' But the mongrel was already there, standing in front of the merchant and smiling by waving his tail. With this merchant Bakkin became confused. He tried to leave but the dog impeded his departure by going behind him and sniffing his shoes. The merchant shivered and turned pale. 'He saw what I was up to,' he said. 'I'm an idiot and a thief,' he continued, 'the fur didn't even belong to me. I borrowed it from my brother and never gave it back.' Now all present began to run away and the cur no longer took up the scent of the thief's track but instead grasped two or three of the nearest fleeing persons. All confessed. One of them had lost money entrusted to him at cards, the second had beaten his wife, and the third had uttered such curses that cannot be repeated here. The crowd was gone. Only the policeman and his cur were left. Then the dog went to the policeman and wagged his tail. The dog handler turned pale, fell on his knees in front of the dog and said: 'Just take me then it's true, I got three dollar for your upkeep and kept two of them for myself.' And how it goes from here, I don't know, because I also got out of there!'

Poor Results

We have seen how, in time, dogs that were trained to follow a track were also used to identify individual people based on the odor of the track. Based on some good results, the faith in dogs being able to point out the guilty person became boundless, and the capacities of dogs were severely overrated. Early last century, the pendulum started to swing back and the work of the dogs was critically reviewed. Finally in 1913 the first people to look at the nose work of the police dogs with a more critical view began to be heard.

The most outspoken criticism came from the Berlin police dog trainer and later Major Konrad Most. In trial he declared to serious doubt that the police dogs were able to work out a five to six hours old track without faults. His statements caused a lot of commotion amongst police dog handlers, and a lot of bitter words were spoken. The Prussian Ministry of the Interior therefore announced a test with the best German police tracking dogs in order to even out the dispute. The Berlin police started testing tracking dogs in 1913 and repeated these tests after the First World War in 1920-1925 and 1927-1930. The results were poor: in following a track the dogs were distracted by cross-tracks and they lost the track altogether when it changed direction. In the same period a number of training-instruction books and theories of how dogs followed a track were published. Success stories and poor results alternated.

Training Method

An interesting controversy about the way that dogs follow a track illustrates the discussion that was taking place at that time of the capabilities of dogs. There were two basic theories that each had its own supporters. According to one theory, the dog follows the individual scent that a person has left on the ground. According to the other theory the dog follows the scent caused by the disturbance of the ground where a person has placed his foot. Experiments conducted by Romanes (1887) and Zell (1909), and the theory of Blunk (1926) supported the first theory: a person leaves his personal odor in his track on the ground and this odor is what the dog follows. Neuhaus (1955) later calculated that for dogs the threshold for butyric acid, a component of human sweat, is low enough for them to easily detect the amount left on the ground by an average footstep. The other theory, which states that dogs base their track on disturbance of the ground was also widely supported: in 1905 Brough concluded that dogs were not able to follow a track once it had been crossed by another. Directors of the German police dog school in Grünheide (Most, 1926; Hansmann, 1931) were convinced of the ability of dogs to discriminate between people on the basis of scent but were unconvinced that this individual odor was in fact the guide for the dogs when following a track. Experiments conducted by the Menzel's in the 1930's and by Schmid in 1937 led to the conclusion that the cue to how the dogs work lies in the way they are trained. The training method should be closely adapted to the exact purpose of the training, and sufficient controls should be built in to test what the dog has learned. With specific training they were able to train dogs to follow the individual human scent on the track (Gerritsen and Haak, 2001.)

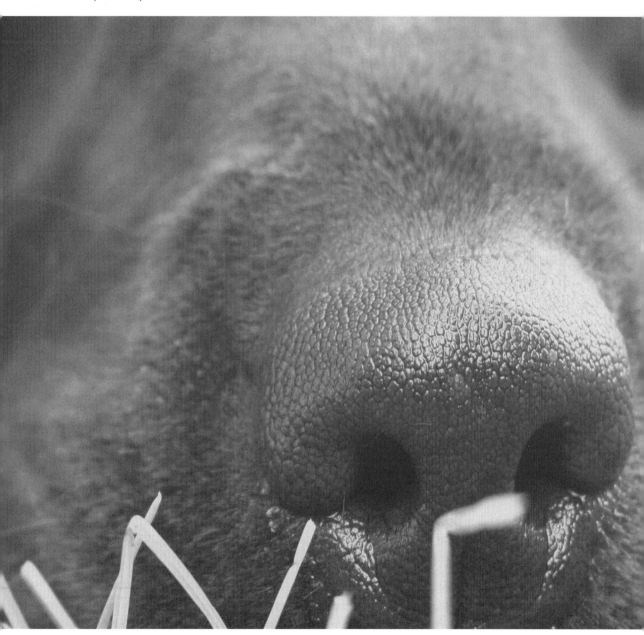

In the 1930's, Dr. Rudolf and Dr. Rudolfina Menzel from Linz (Austria) showed that their dogs were able to follow the individual human scent on track.

Dog Handler Larry Harris (1)

In regards to regulation and protocol of judicial and forensic investigation, the foreknowledge of working towards a certain result dispite whatever the truth may contain is an act of fraudulent investigation.

In 1996 Mr Tony Rackauckas, at that time superior court judge of Orange County in California, made a remarkable decission in a trial involving the brutal murder of an Irvine woman during a burglary. He first allowed the testimony of Larry Harris, a police dog handler who claimed his Bloodhound 'Duchess' indicated the 17-year-old high school student, Earl Henry Rhoney, as the killer. Besides this testimony there was no physical evidence that connected Rhoney to the crime. Quoting R.S Moxley, 2005, after a guilty verdict, Rackauckas shocked the district attorney's office. He declared that Harris lacked credibility and overturned the jury's decision. Without Harris' claim, the district attorney's case collapsed. Rhoney was freed after spending 42 months in jail. According to

Rackauckas, it was 'crystal clear' that Harris had dragged Duchess in Rhoney's direction during identification, that Harris had used a questionable homemade device to allegedly capture Rhoney's scent from the crime scene for the dog, and that the retired McDonnell Douglas engineer-turned-cop-aide was as 'biased as any expert this court has ever seen.'

Dog Handler Larry Harris (2)

About one year the dirt-poor James Ochoa has been locked in a maximum security cell at Theo Lacy Jail, one of Orange County's main jails located in the City of Orange, after in 2005 found guilty without concrete proof; except the controversial evidence of the then 75-year-old Harris and his new Bloodhound 'Trace'.

This is the case as published at the website of the Innocence Project (www.innocenceproject.org): At 12:30 a.m. on May 22, 2005 in Buena Park, California, two young Hispanic men were approached by another young Hispanic male, who pulled out a gun and demanded their wallets and the key to one victim's Volkswagen Jetta. The perpetrator wore a black baseball cap and a flannel

Though police claim that Harris' Bloodhound, Trace, ran directly to Ochoa's front door, the real story is far less incriminating.

shirt. He drove off in the victim's car with $600 from their wallets. The victims immediately called the police. When the responding officer took the description of the perpetrator from the victims, he immediately thought of James Ochoa. Earlier that night, James Ochoa was sitting with two friends outside of his house, which was a few blocks from the robbery. The responding officer had approached them and had searched them, but found no contraband or illegal drugs. Immediately after the victims finished describing the perpetrator, the officer pulled up a picture of James Ochoa on his laptop computer. One victim saw only Ochoa's photograph, while the other saw photographs of Ochoa's two friends (who did not resemble the description just taken) first. Both victims said that the man in the picture 'looked like' the perpetrator.

Just after 1:00 a.m., the stolen Jetta was recovered two blocks from the site of the carjacking, a short distance from Ochoa's house. On the front seat of the locked car was a grey shirt and a black hat. The victims were taken to the car and told the police that the clothing inside belonged to the perpetrator. When the car was towed by police, a black BB gun fell out from under the rear fender. The victims identified the gun as the weapon used by the perpetrator.

At around 3:00 a.m., a Bloodhound dog named 'Trace' was brought to the scene. Over the course of one hour, Trace allegedly followed the scent from a swab from the perpetrator's baseball cap to Ochoa's front door. Ochoa was arrested and the two victims were brought to Ochoa's house around 6:00 a.m.. Ochoa was standing on his front lawn, shirtless and in handcuffs. The victims identified him again and they identified Ochoa a third time two months later in a live lineup.

The black baseball hat, grey shirt, BB gun, and the Jetta's steering wheel cover were all sent to the Orange County Crime Laboratory. Ochoa was eliminated as a possible contributor to DNA on the evidence. More importantly, the major contributor on the baseball hat and on the gun grip exhibited the same unknown male profile. A CODIS database run did not identify the male. A latent fingerprint found on the Jetta's gearshift knob also did not match Ochoa or either victim.

According to news reports, prosecutors attempted to exert pressure on a crime lab analyst who conducted the tests that exonerated Ochoa. The Orange

County Weekly has reported that a deputy district attorney contacted the lab and asked an analyst to change her report – to indicate that Ochoa could have been the perpetrator – before sharing it with Ochoa's defense attorneys. The lab analyst refused to change the report. A judge threatened Ochoa with a sentence of 25 years to life in prison if a jury found him guilty, and against his attorney's advice, Ochoa accepted a plea bargain in December 2005 that led to a sentence of two years in prison.

Quoting R.S. Moxley the weakness of the case is only underscored by Harris' pivotal role in the arrest. Though police claim that Harris' Bloodhound, Trace, ran directly to Ochoa's front door, the real story is far less incriminating. In truth, Trace twice ran by Ochoa's residence without noticing. According to a police report obtained by the Weekly, it wasn't until Harris pointed the dog back toward Ochoa's house that she allegedly ended her hunt there. 'This was the only door she showed any interest in all evening,' Harris wrote. 'It was later confirmed that the subject that lived at that location was involved.' But there are several big problems with Harris' claims:

- Harris claims his dog's identification was solid but failed to note a breach of FBI guidance regarding search dogs: instead of keeping the stolen-car crime scene clean, police swarmed it. Those same officers later surrounded Ochoa's home, and were followed by Trace. It's conceivable, in other words, that Trace had done nothing more than follow the scents of officers she had first picked up around the stolen car.
- The claim that Harris' Bloodhound ran directly to Ochoa's front door doesn't match other descriptions saying Trace twice ran by Ochoa's residence without noticing.
- After that situation a police report declares Harris pointed the dog back toward Ochoa's house.
- Harris description of the dog's scent tracking run of about 50 yards (45 metres) to Ochoa's residence doesn't explain why police logs show it took Trace 63 minutes to find the house.
- Oddly, the cops - satisfied that the dog allegedly tracked a scent to Ochoa's front door - let Harris and Trace leave without identifying Ochoa.

Moxley wrote about this all: It's a catalog of sloppy police work, callous prosecutors, indifferent judges and a brazen contempt for exculpatory evidence. The story would be comical if the consequences weren't so dire.

According to the Innocence Project in October 2006, a man named Jaymes T. McCollum entered the Los Angeles County Jail on unrelated carjacking charges. When McCollum's DNA was entered into CODIS, Buena Park police officer Pete Montez saw that McCollum matched the unknown male profile from Ochoa's case. When Montez confronted him with this information, McCollum confessed to the May 2005 carjacking. The officer informed the Orange County district attorney, who filed a People's Petition for Immediate Habeas Corpus Relief on October 18, 2006. The next day, the same judge who tried Ochoa vacated the conviction. On October 20, 2006, at 6:30AM, correctional officials told Ochoa that he was leaving. Ochoa did not know about the CODIS hit or that his sentence had been vacated. He was not represented by an attorney at the time. He got a ride back to Orange County in a car from the district attorney's office after officials bought him lunch and a set of clothing, sixteen months after he had been arrested for a crime he did not commit...

Signs of the Handler

Influencing of the dog by the handler still is an object. Not only in K9's but also in hobby examinations. Lots of dogs pass their tracking examinations after being led by their handler over the track. Just like search dogs, such as detector dogs or search and rescue dogs, that react at signs of the handler, because the handler knows where something or someone is hidden. That in this way trained dogs in difficult situations, f.i. at a real mission, fail is logical and can be expected.

The only way to avoid such problems is, as soon as the dog knows the technique of tracking or searching, to work 'blind' that is, the handler doesn't know the course of the track or the hiding place. And never forget the influence which an instructor, or other people present, unintentional have on the dog.

Deliberately

Also Prof. David Katz of the Stockholm University emphatically points out that 'as well the tough practice of K9's as those of the sports dog will never reach a higher level as long as we don't understand the influence of the 'Clever Hans' effect and fool ourselves, handling the dog wrong and we on his turn let ourselves cheat by the dog. Tracking only make a sense if the handler doesn't know the path of the track. Everything else is only a childish fool yourself and tracking, also for a dog, absolutely unworthy.'

Tracking only makes sense if the handler doesn't know the path of the track.

The ethologists were in their time the first to tell the police dog handlers they made the Clever Hans fault. Unintentional the handler led his dog on the track, and not the dog the handler. That mostly happened unconscious with little body movements, signs, encouragement and movements with the tracking leash. And sometimes also conscious because the handler knew who was suspected and where he lived...

Dog Handler John Preston

Former Pennsyslvania Highway Patrol Trooper John Preston already mentioned at the beginning of this chapter claimed in the 80's of the former century performances of his dog that verges on the incredible. And in fact were incredible, because not only he lied on oath about the training of his dogs but also he rigged lots of search acts. Preston, now deceased, travelled with his dogs all over the United States in order to solve big criminal cases and lots of convictions based on the fancied 'proofs' of his dog. Their reliance on Preston put innocent

It wasn't the fault of Preston's dogs - they were simply used by him as a glory-producing tool for shameless self-promotion.

men on Death Row and wrecked multiple lives.

Gilbert Goshorn, a former Brevard County Judge, designed a test in 1984 to determine whether Preston's dog could do what it purported to do. Goshorn's test of the dog handler's scent-tracking ability involved two lawyers jogging down separate paths. The following morning, the dog was given one lawyer's sweat-soaked shirt to see if the dog could follow the trail. The dog failed. Goshorn told Preston that he would give him a second chance a day later, but the handler and his dog left town and never testified in Brevard again.

'It is my belief that the only way Preston could achieve the results he achieved in numerous other cases was having obtained information about the case prior to the scent tracking so that Preston could lead the dog to the suspect or evidence in question,' Goshorn continued in his affidavit. 'I believe that Preston was regularly retained to confirm the state's preconceived notions about a case.'

Prosecutors, including ones in Brevard, continued using Preston's services after a 1983 federal investigation initiated by the U.S. Postal Service. It said Preston routinely asked investigators for information about a case before using the dog and that he led his dog to supply wanted results.

Preston's cases were overturned in Arizona, where the state's highest court referred to him as a 'charlatan' and Geraldo Rivera exposed the con job on national TV in 1984.

Titusville attorney and former Brevard prosecutor Sam Bardwell, who encountered Preston in a 1981 rape case, says then-State Attorney Doug Cheshire as well as the Brevard Sheriff's Office and most law enforcement officers at the time knew Preston was a charlatan. 'I left the State Attorney's Office because I could not abide by the fabrication of evidence,' Bardwell says. 'Fabrication of evidence' are serious charges. And in the case of Preston, proven. But the false trackings and testimonies aren't stopped of since...

K9 Fraud!

Chapter 4:
Scent Research and Tracking Experiments

One of the biggest problems in all scent work is that humans lack the sensitivity of the dog's nose, and dogs lack the human's interest in certain scents. Ordinarily a dog pays attention to completely different items than we do. A lot of things we do not pay attention to, or even turn up our nose to (sometimes literally, because it stinks so much) are, for the dog, of great importance – enough to study them more closely. It is good to know these differences in observations between humans and dogs; that way we can better understand the behavior of dogs during search work. Because of a difference in interest, our world and that of a dog's looks different. This was described very clearly by German Professor Dr. J. von Uexküll.

Human World

A HUMAN AND HIS DOG walk together in a town. The handler passes a clothes shop and is very interested in clothes displayed there. Then, he goes by a jewelers, where rings and watches lay in the shop window. At last he stops at a bookstore, where he looks at books and magazines. He pays less attention to the butcher shop, after which he walks around a corner into a park, on a staircase to a terrace, where he sits on a chair and looks at the nice flowerbeds around him.

Dog World

The dog experiences the world totally differently when he goes out for this walk with his owner. He passes the clothes shop; the things displayed there don't interest him. These only become of interest when the owner or another housemate has worn them and they have absorbed the body odor. Our watches and books also don't interest him. The display for him is nothing more than an unimportant mess of lines and surfaces. The butcher shop says more to him. The odor of meat and sausages sparks his appetite and the odor of waste makes him want to roll in it. Also very important for him, is the stone on the corner of the street. Every male that has passed there planted a more or less strong odor. He has to study these very seriously, and after he has added his, he could continue his walk. The staircase of the terrace is like walking up a hill, and he may not even notice that the slope is interrupted by stairs. The rail of the staircase is for him unimportant, but the cushions of the chairs interest him. Of the beauty of the flowerbed, he probably sees nothing; the park only gets his attention when he sees a mouse running by.

The Human world v.s. The Dog world. Only the items in black play a role in the dog's world; all the other items, important in the human world - the books, paintings, mirror, table, lamp, bottle, glasses etc., have no place in the dog's world.

Different Worlds

Because of this difference in interests, humans live in a totally different world from dogs. His interest is much more determined than ours and is, as with every animal, limited to what is considered a vital importance to them. There is a question whether a dog really observes the mirror on the wall of the living room, the table and cupboards, or if he just walks around them mechanically. Of the things on the table, the plates will get his attention if they are filled with food. Does he ever notice the sky or the tops of the trees as anything other than background to a couple of flying ducks, or to a cat escaping into a tree? Does he note the singing of the birds, although his sense of hearing is very good? Does he distinguish between the odors of flowers? If he is trained for it, he can do that, but ordinarily? All such things lay outside his sphere of interest. His world is not only different, but also much smaller than ours. Humans and dogs live in qualitatively different worlds, however closely we live in the same surroundings. What the dog perceives is not a coincidence, but depends largely on the attention, and the interest of the animal. This will happen when there is a sense of biological meaning for the dog, that is, an object that plays an obvious role in the dog's life. The odor of other dogs is an example of this, as is the observation of a cat or hearing the barking of another dog. The attention given a certain perception can also be decided by experience. The reaction of the dog on noticing the approach of a person or animal he recognizes by the odor or sound, are examples of perceptions heightened through attention. Also through training, the dog can be become interested in perceptions, which for an untrained dog lay far under the perception level.

Prickle Thresholds

There is also the question of whether the senses of a dog are strongly divided from each other as they are with humans. The dog is used to combine seeing and smelling in many cases. He probably possesses another prickle threshold for those sensory perceptions that naturally cooperate, opposed to those that are separately stimulated. That's why it is very illogical to suppose that tracking dogs only use their nose and don't search with their eyes for soil damage or changes in the terrain.

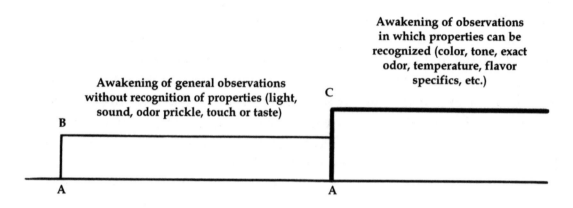

Schematic representation of the absolute (A-B) and specific (A-C) prickle threshold.

It is imperative to first know something about the concepts of prickle threshold and threshold value: it is impossible to understand the discussion about scent and search work if you are not familiar with the ingenious system of the prickle threshold. This concept is based on the familiar image of a house – which the awareness lives in a ground floor room, and anything approaching the awareness, like a visitor to the house, first has to step over the threshold of the house before coming into the presence of the awareness. Conversely, the higher the room or awareness, the higher the threshold to step over to enter the room and, of course, the stronger the prickle has to be to step over the threshold to penetrate the awareness.

The threshold value, in any given case, is the prickle strength just needed to cross the threshold and penetrate the awareness. We can imagine crossing the threshold in two ways: one, which the prickle is just strong enough for us to get the message that it exists; two, that the prickle is so strong that we can observe certain qualities about it.

Because humans are most familiar with sight impressions, this very important difference will be explained using the example of the human eye. A weak beam of light can be just strong enough for the human eye to observe the existence of the light without noticing any other details about it. We then would say that this beam of light has passed the absolute prickle threshold. As the light slowly becomes brighter, sooner or later the eye would begin to observe the properties of this light, for instance its color. This is passing the specific prickle threshold.

The same, of course, is true of the sense of smell. An odor (for instance on a very old human track) can be just strong enough to be observed by a tracking dog as a track; however, the odor may no longer be strong enough to give the dog particular information about it, such as the specific odor of the tracklayer. The strength of the odor is above the absolute, but under the specific prickle threshold.

Various Levels

Anyone who has observed living humans and animals knows that you have to pay close attention to the fact that the prickle threshold is not a rigid and uniform sensation. Different creatures have different high prickle thresholds. There are, for instance, dogs who will follow any approaching stranger and bark, while other dogs will let a stranger into the house without any fuss at all. Between these two there are various levels, and even the same creature doesn't always have the same level of prickle threshold. There are a lot of factors that can influence the strength of a prickle threshold. Health, way of life, reception, acquaintance, interest, hunger, training, and tiredness, all can affect the threshold. Someone who takes good care of himself knows that at different times he will react differently to prickles coming to him from the outside. Depending on circumstances, we say of ourselves that we are in a good or bad mood, happy or sad, irritated or nervous. That means our prickle threshold is under the influence of these factors and can be change substantially in terms of levels.

We know something similar about the dog. Anyone who has spent time observing them knows that dogs can also be in a good or bad mood, which can alter their prickle threshold in a positive or negative way. The nose of the dog, its finest instrument, is particularly sensitive, especially when we demand a higher performance. Here a lot of factors can play a disturbing role in whether the odor can reach the absolute or specific prickle threshold, to the point of failing to cross the threshold altogether.

Perception

The problem with using a dog's nose for our detection and tracking work, is not just a physiological one – a question of the capabilities of the nasal organ itself – but is also a psychological problem, depending on the dog's intelligence and ability to learn, and the attention of the dog and its present prickle threshold.

Sensory perception is not an easy process, but a combination of different factors. In order for the dog to make a sensory perception, he must have a fully functioning and well-built registration system (eye, ear, nose, etc.) From these organs there must be a healthy nerves system to connect to the brain. Again, this has to function very well. So each part of the system must be functioning properly in order for an accurate perception to be made. Then there has to be, for that sense, a specific and sufficiently strong prickle and, at last, the dog's attention must be directed to this prickle. Only when all these factors are operating can the dog perceive.

Tiredness

This view cannot go without mentioning the effects of tiredness. These effects can play a very important, sometimes a deciding, role in perception. Tiredness can strike at each of the mentioned factors of perception. In the nose, for instance, the time it takes to breathe out has to be long enough for the mucous membrane to recover. The same is true of the nerves, which have to be able to carry the prickle to the brain. Physical tiredness can show up in search work or tracking, particularly on longer tracks. For that reason, it is not advisable to do any tiring work with the dog just before tracking. For best results in tracking, as in every form of search work, it is best to start with a physically well-rested dog!

In dogs, the mental tiredness – the fatigue of the brain – plays an important part. Mental tiredness can sometimes be seen in very long and difficult tracks, especially when the odor is close to the prickle threshold, or sometimes even under it, so that the dog has to work extra hard over the parts where there is no odor, and hence no prickle. Mental tiredness can also occur when the dog has to work a long time, especially when it is very warm or if the dog is under pressure (from the handler, change of surroundings, unusual travel, etc.) The dog will then, in spite of a normal effort, deliver poor results. Tiredness can also be expressed by reduced attention: the dog slows down, is not interested in the track or search work, is diverted by any little thing, is catching flies, is relieving himself, and so on. You can overcome this tiredness by getting the dog's attention back on tracking or search work.

Prickle Summarizing

In their book the philosopher Dr. Rudolfina Menzel and her husband, the physician Dr. Rudolf Menzel, summarized the very important concept for tracking odors. A prickle that is too weak by itself to be perceived (and is thus under the absolute threshold value) can become more noticeable if it is constantly and continuously picked up. Though separate, the weak prickles following each other will summarize. When these prickles are summarized, they can cross the absolute and even the specific prickle threshold. The last prickle to overcome the threshold of awareness isn't the strongest itself, but by accumulation has become a sort of ladder, allowing a weak prickle to cross a higher threshold.

It's like having a small pain, for example a headache – normally we don't discover the pain suddenly. It isn't that the pain becomes more severe, but only that the pain prickles have summarized and come slowly to our awareness.

Another example to make this clearer is to picture being asleep when the alarm goes off. You're so deeply asleep that at first, you don't notice the alarm. Even in sleep, our prickle threshold is so high that even a loud, piercing tone cannot cross the threshold. The alarm continues to ring, so at last the noise summarizes into prickles that can cross the absolute prickle threshold, so we hear the noise in our sleep, but don't necessarily recognize it. It's not unusual to dream of fire alarms and sirens until the prickle manages to cross the specific prickle threshold, when we recognize the well-known tone, which most of us don't like so much, and awaken.

It is unbelievably important in understanding the work of the tracking dog well to first understand this summarizing effect and to use it in training our dogs. For instance, in older tracks the amount of human odor in one footstep can be under the specific prickle threshold, not enough to be perceived by the dog. Only through the summation of the odor prickles is it possible for the tracking dog to perceive anything about the odor quality of the tracklayer. However, the summation of prickles doesn't have to take place without interruption. Frequent repetition at certain intervals between prickles can strengthen weak prickles enormously. This is also the secret of the advertising world; that a one-time ad can go unnoticed, because it doesn't grab our attention, but the same ad confronting us daily will work its way into our distracted brains. In the same way, a certain human odor can, by repetition, work its way into the dog's perception.

Systematic Training

In general tracking or search dog training, the biggest mistake is that it is accepted that the dog, from the beginning, knows what humans expect of him. They believe that the dog will be instantly interested in any odor the handler wants him to be interested in, and that he will concentrate automatically on that odor. They unconsciously think that it is as simple as giving the dog the order to sit or to lie down. But the work of searching and tracking, unlike the simple command-response training, requires more systematic training that has to go in two directions at once.

First, the handler must bring the dog's attention to focus on sense impressions which is something the dog would never be interested by himself. The second task is to train the dog to respond to key words, which can help to bridge this gap between the handler's needs and the dogs understanding.

In no other part of dog training or career is the bond between handler and dog as clearly visible as with search work. Here you can't achieve anything by violence or pressure. Only a good understanding between handler and dog can it possible to achieve success. With search work, we must be willing to follow the dog in his world, and to recognize his superiority in this area.

Chapter 4

The idea of search work is to increase the access of our own sense organs, through the use of another creatures' - to a world that should really be closed to us forever: The world of odors.

Lost Knowledge

For more than a century, people have been researching the ability of dogs and their sense of smell. What followed was thousands of tracks and countless scent tests, some conducted by such pioneer researchers as Most, Brückner, Böttger, Hansmann, Belleville and the Menzels. The accumulation of these successful experiments gave us the knowledge we now have about scent training. It is, however, a pity that a lot of present-day handlers, instructors and even judges don't know (or disregard) all the valuable and very useful results of these tests. Knowledge of this would increase the general quality of our tracking, trailing and detector dogs, as well in dog's engaged in sports!

The First Tracking Tests

In the 19th century, G.J. Romanes researched the ability of the dog to follow human footsteps. He described in 1887 how his dog, a Setter, could follow his track even though it was covered with the tracks of eleven other people. Romanes performed his experiments in 1885 and published the results two years later in the important scientific magazine titled 'Nature'. His results, however, were not quantified and all the tests were done with his own Setter, which had a strong bond to Romanes.

While his dog was held by a helper, Romanes walked in his hunting costume into a shooting ground. After walking for about a mile, he disappeared out of sight, and the helper set loose the Setter. It hurled itself with full enthusiasm and enormous speed on the track of its handler and very soon caught up with him. Even when Romanes rubbed his shoes with aniseed oil, giving the track a strong aniseed odor, the Setter followed his track after only some hesitation.

In another test, Romanes placed eleven people one behind the other and then stood in front of the line. The group moved and everyone had to step in the footsteps of the person who walked in front of them. After about one hundred and eighty meters, Romanes turned with five helpers behind him to the right, while the six others went to the left. His Setter was brought to the shooting ground and began to track. At the place where they had split into two grounds, the dog walked on in search for more intensive signs of the direction of Romanes and quickly located the correct track to the right. With that it was accepted that dogs were able to find and work out a track of his handler out of a mix of twelve, and later on out of six different tracks.

However, the dog was not succeeding in working out the track of a stranger. After that, Romanes decided to exchange his boots with those of a stranger and both laid tracks. The dog worked out the track laid by the stranger – who wore the boots of his handler – very intensively, but he didn't pick up the track of his handler with the stranger's boots; even when he was encouraged to do so.

Romanes continued his tests and laid a track in socks he had worn for a while. The dog didn't pick up this track either, but when Romanes laid a track in bare feet, his dog worked it out, although slowly and with some hesitation. When his handler was wearing new boots, the dog couldn't localize the track.

Continuing his experiments, he glued brown paper into the soles and sides of his old boots and laid a track. At the beginning, the Setter didn't pay much attention to the track, but that changed when he came on a place where a piece of paper was loosened from the heel of the boot. The dog recognized the track of his handler, and followed it cheerfully, even though this little piece of paper was only a few millimeters squared.

Romanes assumed that the dog was not just working out the track of his handler, but those of his hunting boots; a composite scent consisting of the leather of the boots and the odor of his feet. The dog could, however, very clearly distinguish the odor of his handler from that of the boots, as proved by another experiment. Romanes walked about the first fifty meters on his boots, then almost three hundred meters in his socks and after that, the same distance in his bare feet. His dog worked out the track until the end, by which Romanes concluded that the dog, after first following the mix of scents, could recognize a single part of it and also could follow this single part. This all was worked out correctly by the dog as long as it was his handler's track, but the Setter didn't succeed on the tracks of strangers.

The results of these experiments weren't well known in the beginning of the twentieth century, especially not by the police, who at that time fully trusted the dog and accepted the results of the dog as convincing evidence – even though it was often obtained by influence from the handler or the possible suspect. At that time, the capabilities of police tracking dogs were quite overrated, given the knowledge and training available, and that led to many dubious results.

Systematically Research

The first person to systematically research the tracking of dogs, and published on the subject, was Dr. Friedo Schmidt from Stralsund, Germany. In 1910, he described how the substances that contains human odor immediately, or soon after the shoes touches the ground, form a smell-able track for the dog. He noted that the physical condition of the dog could negatively impact on tracking. This could be because of poor food or long travelling. He also proved that trying to hide the individual odor or to lay an 'odorless track' with new shoes made tracking more difficult for the dog, but that it was not impossible.

In spite of the clear results of his research, Schmidt pointed out that a successful track by a police dog must be seen only as an indication and not as evidence. Dr. Schmidt's caution did not hold sufficient weight, so before and after the First World War, there were intense discussions about the value of the police dog when tracking criminals. The Prussian Minister of the Interior asked well-known police dog trainer, and later major, Konrad Most for his advice about this matter.

Most's Tracking Cross

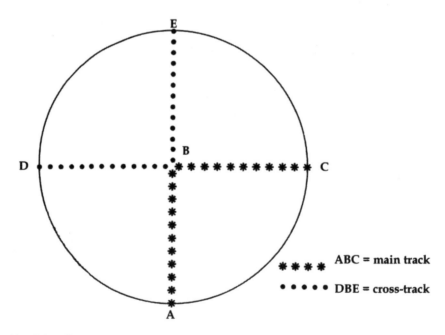

Most's Tracking Cross. One of the most difficult tracking
exercises for a dog is to follow track ABC. In many tests,
dogs tracked correctly from A to B, but at the cross-track
went there over to E.

Chapter 4

Konrad Most had many police tracking dogs available for his research. After he proved that a dog could easily move over from one track to another, he investigated the cause and conditions under which a dog might follow the wrong track. His research concerned two questions: 'What is an odor track for the dog and which odors lead the dog?' and 'How long is it possible for the dog to follow track laid by a human in shoes?'

After countless tests, Konrad Most developed a tracking scheme that became known as Most's Tracking Cross. In this, one tracklayer walks from point A to C, and another tracklayer from point D to E, and meeting each other at point B. The dog starts at A and is supposed to track to C, with D, B, and E offering a tempting cross-track. Because all the dogs, arriving at B followed the track to E or made other mistakes, in 1914 Most concluded that dogs are not able to follow the individual human odor in a track; they are not 'track-sure'. Also he concluded that dogs cannot recognize articles with the odor of the tracklayer on the basis of the odor of the track, and dogs can only follow tracks that are no more than five hours old.

Repeating the Tests

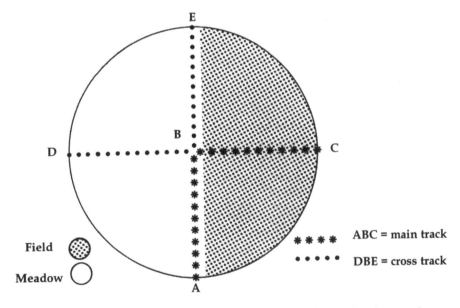

Most's Tracking Cross with a change in terrain is much more difficult for the dog.

Because of the First World War, Konrad Most had to stop his research on tracking dogs; however, in 1920, Most repeated his earlier tests with the best tracking dogs of that time. The result was, as it was before, disappointing and proved that the tested dogs were not track-sure. With the presence of a cross-track in strange terrain, the dogs always went astray.

In another test thirteen trained dogs were used, one of them a gundog, of which the owners were convinced that they could recognize and follow the track of their handler among other tracks. The fifty two tests showed ten correct and forty two wrong results; no single dog did everything correct, but only as often as could be expected by the probability of these figures. With the presence of only a single strange track in the field, the dogs often followed the wrong track and didn't find their handler. There were cross-tracks in each of these tests – which presented serious difficulties. Animals are tempted a lot more easily than humans, as animals only focus on their senses and their attention, and don't have a rational or critical consciousness.

With cross-tracks, the angle to the main track is also important. If the turn is much less than ninety degrees to the track, dogs can hardly go over on it. If the turn, however, is much more than ninety degrees, so forming an obtuse angle to the track, then there's a greater chance that the dog will go over to the cross-track, especially when the cross-tracks are fresher.

One of the most difficult tasks for a tracking dog is to follow a track connected to Most's Tracking Cross. It becomes harder still when there is also a change from one terrain in another. For example, if a track changes from a meadow into a field. The tests with Most's Tracking Cross, even according to Konrad Most himself, are among the hardest exercises for a tracking dog.

Disagreements

The publication of Most's research lead to very serious disagreements, because supporters of the use of police tracking dogs, like criminologist Paul Böttger and veterinarian Dr. J. Hansmann from Berlin, felt the work of these dogs were being threatened. They could prove in practice much better results than Most's tests showed. Physiological and psychological factors in the work of the tracking dog were not sufficiently accounted for in the discussions, so there was a lot of misunderstanding.

Given the training techniques of that time, in the opinion of Konrad Most, the police tracking dogs only followed the physical changes to the ground surface, namely the evaporation of sap from damaged plants and rotting bacteria. In his view, dogs were not track-reliable, particularly for psychological reasons. On the other hand, German researchers Dr. J. Hansmann, Paul Böttger and Dr. R. Blunk, just like Dr. Rudolf and Rudolfina Menzel, believed that human odors, transferred to the ground were leading the tracking dog.

Extensive Experiments

Extensive tests followed: Konrad Most and Dr. G.H. Brückner, between 1927 and 1930, did as many as 1 268 tracking tests. Major R. Belleville conducted a total of 1 458 tracks, with 4 404 cross-tracks between 1930 and 1935. Dr. J. Hansmann and Paul Böttger declared that, between 1925 and 1932, they tested 'many thousands' of tracks in the German Police Dog School of Grünheide.

After 1930, Konrad Most continued his experiments. With a cable-lift he developed and a big wheel with wooden and porcelain shoes attached, he laid tracks without human odor. In earlier tests, he used this cable to pull a person close above the ground's surface, without touching the ground.

Control Test

The first tests with the cable-lift were conducted with four well-trained police tracking dogs. All dogs were first put through a control test, as described by Most:

A test person walked from point A to B and back to point A. The dog started to track at A. All dogs tracked from point A to B, circled the end point, without walking past the end of the track, as a lot of poorly trained dogs do. At point B the dogs weren't called back, yet they tracked back to point A on their own.

Air-Transferred Odors

Konrad Most's float apparatus, by which the tracklayer was pulled forward just above the ground.

First, tests were done to answer the question of whether odors from a person suspended above the ground fall down on the track. This was, and still is the solution that is accepted. In 1958 R.J. Clifford, and after him W.G. Syrotuck in 1972, published the theory that flakes of skin fall from the human body and so form an important odor track for the dog. In the time of Konrad Most, it was thought that 'odor substances' fall down from someone whether they be walking, on stilts, or riding a bicycle. These substances float in the air or lay on the ground.

The deciding test was worked out by Most and goes as follows:

A test person walks the distance from point A to B, where he sits on the plank of the machine that will suspend him in the air. Then, he is transported further while his feet are about thirty centimeters above the ground. Immediately after that, the dog was placed at point A on the track. In all tests, the dogs tracked only as far as point B (as they did in the control test,) and returned to point A after searching. All attempts to teach the dog to track a human who was moved above the ground failed.

It is for sure, Konrad Most concluded, that human odor substances falling from above do not produce enough of a track for the dog to follow.

In response to this test Dr. F.J.J. Buytendijk made the following remark:

Besides the footprints, if the track of a human also contains odor substances that fall down to the ground, then it is possible that this total odor complex is what leads the dog, not the odors falling down alone. Most's test does not totally exclude the possibility that, in the normal human track, odors falling from above have a meaning in the whole smell impression. However, the test indicates very well that, under these circumstances and within the confines of the test, such odors don't produce by themselves a track that a dog can work out. Even waving arms and legs while riding on Most's float apparatus didn't bring better results of the dogs.
Time could be a factor in these tests, because the dogs were put on the track almost immediately. Dust particles and flakes of skin float in the air and need a certain amount of time to reach the ground. Wind can also cause them to fall up to a few meters beside the track. But even in our own experiments, on much older tracks, we didn't succeed in getting the dogs to work out the part of the track that continued under a float apparatus, not even when the person on the float apparatus was dragged very slowly and only a few centimeters above the ground.

Drops of saps

In a next test, Konrad Most hung cans filled with sap and juice on the cable-lift. The human track was continued with these completely different odors slowly dripping from the cans; however, the police tracking dogs couldn't follow such tracks. The dogs could follow the canned tracks, if the cans contained meat juices or blood. It is clear, that these tracks must have a biological meaning for the dog – that is, the odor of meat, game, female dog in heat, etc.

Konrad Most's dropping cans.

Tracks without Human Odor

Finally, Most did tests with a tracking wheel, on which were affixed wooden, and later on porcelain, shoes. When the human track was continued by this wheel, with the human track layer still being transported on the floating apparatus in another direction, even the best police dog followed the tracks made by the wheel. For Most, it was clear that the damage to the ground's surface and the odors of the plants determined important information for the dog his tracking. The addition of the human odors, according to Most, only added to a part of the total odor complex.

How right it is, as Most said later on, that a dog can find his way back to his handler based on knowledge of the handlers habits or by following the freshest track – but such a statement is not valid in every case. If there is only one track in a given terrain, the dog may follow it without ever perceiving the specific human odor. In such a case, the dog can very easily go to the track of another person. The question then became how far the dog will overshoot the false track. In Most's test, the artificial track was about 128 paces, and rather short. In Romanes' tests, we saw that the Setter first overshot the branching of the tracks.

We also can observe these habits in ourselves; when we're absent-minded or distracted we sometimes walk or drive down the wrong street without noticing. It may take some time before we discover we've made a mistake. How often have you gone all the way home without thinking about it? To suppose that a dog naturally focuses his attention on the track all the time is illogical. Of course, it is possible to teach a dog to focus his attention for a certain time on the track. That requires a strong bond with the dog to pass on this stimulus. It is also important to vary the tracking, by changing terrain and conditions.

Clean-scent Tracking

Most's tests indicated that dogs will follow the track laid by the porcelain shoes as if they were a human track, and that by using the float apparatus, without touching the ground, there was

Konrad Most made artificial tracks with a tracking wheel with wooden shoes, and later, with porcelain shoes.

no track that the dog could follow. This confirmed Most's earlier opinion that tracking dogs follow the mixture of odors from the damaged ground, plants and of our shoes.

But even before 1930, Dr. Blunk and the Menzel doctors, as well as later police dog handlers from Munich, had demonstrated clean-scent tracking on strange odors. By laying tracks with bare feet over an ice surface, Dr. Hansmann in 1931 proved that the skin of the feet produced a very good track to follow.

Whether or not dogs could be trained to recognize and to follow these odors of the tracklayer, out of the total odor complex of the track, kept Most busy in a high measure. Around 1930, after a lot of training, he did indeed succeed in teaching some dogs to stay on the track of their handler, even when these tracks were approached closely and even crossed-over by cross-tracks. But it was a lot more difficult for him to make a dog track-sure on the tracks of a stranger.

To clarify on Most's methods, he didn't use a start point – that is, a place at the beginning of the track with higher odor content. After he made such starts, his results were immediately much better. Because of the stronger odor at the start, the dog gave more attention to the track he had to follow. On top of that, the other cross-tracks and the difference between the younger and older tracks were suddenly a lot less interesting to the dog.

R. Belleville, in 1938, gave the final assessment:

> The secret was, besides another training method, to create a starting point on a track, something that hasn't been done until now. At the beginning of the track, there should be a spot of about half a meter square, created by someone standing there for a period of time to leave extra odor. If the dog can pick up enough of the odor and under normal conditions, then it could be proven that within 86 % to 97 % certainty that the dog will follow the individual's odor on the track. The certainty that the dog would not be fooled by a cross-track was 100 %, if the difference in time between both tracks was at least ten minutes. Even at a time difference of three minutes, there was still a reasonable certainty that the dog would stay on the track.

Influence of Fatty Acids

The influences of the fatty acids, which are present in human sweat, on tracking were tested by Dr. T. Uchida from Japan. In 1953, he used the best

Japanese tracking dogs to work out tracks, which were laid according to Most's Tracking Cross method. He assessed the results of these well-trained German Shepherds, and through this process, he selected the best dogs.

For the next tests the tracks were polluted with butyric acid: Tracklayer A wore shoes which contained traces of butyric acid until they made a turn, and then he put on his own shoes. The shoes of tracklayer B were normal until the same turn, and that time butyric acid was added. All dogs correctly followed the track of A, even at the turn, and were not tempted to go over to the tracks of B.

During a similar test, a mixture of fatty acids and other substances present in human sweat were used instead of butyric acid. From that moment on, the dogs followed the polluted track and crossed from track A to track B. Also, there were some dogs which refused to work out the track at all.

These experiments proved that a good dog can not only recognize the qualitative and quantitative details of a human sweat, but can also use them as a guide for tracking; and that the dog is not tempted away from the track by the alteration of one single odor component. Only when multiple odor components are changed or used as a distraction can the dog no longer with certainty determine the details of the odor track, which, is to be expected.

Y-scheme Tracks

The ability of dogs to determine the differences in odors between a main track and a cross-track, was again tested in 1967 during the doctoral research of Dr. J. Honhon from Paris. He didn't use Most's Tracking Cross, but a Y-scheme. At the branch of the Y, the dogs had to decide which track they should follow, the original track or the cross-track.

Honhon determined that the right choice was depending on the length of the track between the start and the cross track, and on the gap in time between the creation of the main track and the cross-track.

If the first leg was eight hundred meters long, then 75 – 85 % of the time the dogs stayed on the correct track; if it was only fifty meters long, then the dogs chose the correct way in only 45 % of the time.

If the difference in time between the creation of the main track and the cross-track was a quarter of an hour, then in 65 – 75 % of the cases the dogs made the correct choice. If this difference in time was half an hour, then the correct decision was made in 70 – 75 % of the dogs. Finally, if this difference was one hour, then in 75 – 85 % of the cases the main track was followed.

Honhon's research confirmed the conclusions of the Austrian and German research of the late thirties.

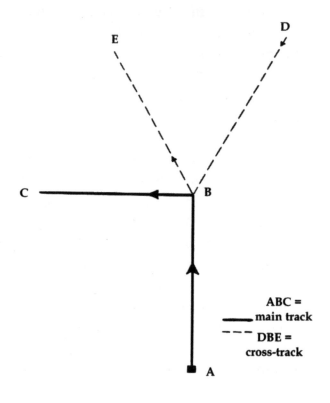

The Y-scheme of Honhon. Staying on the track from A to C depends on the length from A to B and the difference in time with cross-track D-E. The greater these are the more chance the dog tracks from A to C.

Breathing and Scanning Odors

In his dissertation on the smelling ability of dogs, Dr. Karl Zuschneid in 1973, used electronic measuring equipment. Thanks to these, Dr. Zuschneid could obtain measurements of respiration in tracking dogs for his physiological research. The registration of respiration during tracking was observed by the movement of the breath in the middle of the nostrils. Two small plastic tubes were placed in the nostrils that transported a part of the air flow to the measuring equipment.

First Dr. Zuschneid did tests without equipment, by which he could also determine how long tracks were perceptible to the dogs under certain weather conditions. He also wanted to clarify whether the fatty acids, and the fatty acid mixes, by themselves (without the odors of the tracklayer), formed a smell-able track for the dog. Therefore, he used different fatty acids and fatty acid mixes, like butyric, proprionic, formic, acetic and caprionic acid.

In total five German Wirehaired Pointers were tested on sixty tracks with lengths from seven hundred to one thousand meters. The research showed that, with tracks under different conditions, the shortest perceptible time was measured on a dry, dusty field, while the longest perceptible time, more than twenty two hours, took place in a deciduous wood at autumn with a relative humidity of 70 to 90 %.

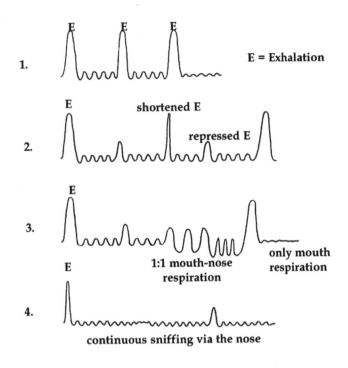

Zuschneid's four phases of sniffing. The basic pattern will change from 1 to 4 with more difficult tracks.

Furthermore, all the dogs showed great interest in fatty acids, although this clearly depended on the concentration and the composition of the fatty acid mix. The dogs could convincingly and without problems follow a twenty four hour old tracks of a 1/40 mol. dilution (1/40 gram molecule per liter) butyric acid.

The registration of the dog's respiration during tracking showed a characteristic picture, more or less, the same in all dogs. The sniffing of the dog was printed on paper as waves that were regularly interrupted by exhalation. That way a sniffing frequency and a length of the sniffing period could be determined. The sniffing period is the duration of uninterrupted characteristic sniffing inspiration between exhalation gusts via the nose. Four basic patterns could be determined:

1. For simple tracks (for instance, thirty minute old tracks of the handler under favorable conditions) the picture was one of regular sniffing inhalations. The waves of the pressure differences are often small, which means that the speed of air movement in the nose is low. The exhalation gusts via the nose are powerful and regular. In almost all simple tracks this respiration picture was consistent from beginning to end of the track.

2. The above respiration picture fades away when the track increases in difficulty. The waves of exhalation become smaller and the time between them increases. In other words, the dog sniffs longer, creating more air pressure in the nose.

3. The next phase shows the same picture as the preceding in principle. The sniffing periods are, however, still longer and there are short, characteristic periods in which the dog is obviously breathing through mouth and nose. It wasn't unusual to see some dogs exhale via the nose in double gusts.

4. Finally, in the difficult parts of tracking, the respiration showed the dog was almost continuously sniffing. A female dog showed the longest period, a respiration pattern over eighty seconds long.

Exhaling probably performs a sort of cleaning of the cells in the nose mucous membrane, which is apparently less necessary for lower odor concentrations. It looks as though dogs breathe reacted in the same way as they do with panting in warm temperatures. But unlike panting, which is mostly ventilation without breathing, here the high frequency of sniffing indeed contributes to the inhalation.

On simple tracks dogs succeed easily in combining breathing and scanning for odors. The inhalation takes place during the sniffing.

When the odor of the track decreases, then the dog solves this problem in two ways: The speed of the air intake increases, by which the capacity grows. The dog also extends the total duration of the sniffing. The delayed exhalation then takes place partly via the nose and partly via the slightly open mouth. The inclination to delay exhaling is a disadvantage for breathing. But it creates an advantage in getting, by longer sniffing, more information about the incoming odors.

When the difficulty of the track increases due to extreme conditions, exhalation is suppressed altogether. During tracks with minimum odor, exhalation more often takes place via the mouth. The lesser resistance and the larger opening of the mouth allows for greater air volumes to pass than by exhalation through the nose. Because of that, exhalation takes less time. So, tracking with an open mouth is an advantage that it saves time in sniffing and scanning for odors.

Sniffing

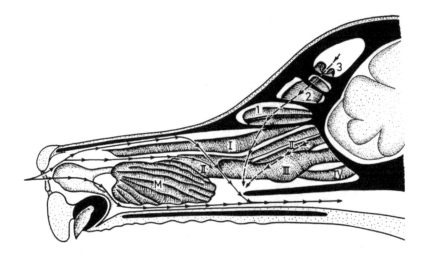

Air current in the dog's nose. The unbroken line is the inhaled air. A negative pressure arises behind the conchae maxillaris (M). The air flow (interrupted line) from the sinuses (1, 2 and 3) and the conchae ethmoidalis (I-IV) eliminates the differences in pressure.

In 1981, Prof. Dr. Walter Neuhaus wrote about the importance of sniffing for the olfaction of the dog. Sniffing for dogs consists of a series of eight to twenty short puffs of inhalation followed by one exhalation. During a single puff of inhalation no whirls are formed in the nasal cavity, as was thought in the past. The space between the nasal turbinate is too small. The small amount and low speed of the air sucked in stays under the critical value for current turbulence. The inhaled air reaches the rear parts of the olfactory mucous membrane in the sinuses by differences in pressure in the nose.

Due to the considerable negative pressure from behind the Conchae Maxillaris during inhalation, air is drawn from the spaces between the Conchae Ethmoidalis and from the frontal sinuses. At the end of the inhalation, scented air flows back into these spaces, so that even the parts of the olfactory epithelium located in the frontal sinuses and remote from the breathing flow are stimulated. During a single sniff, diffusion is of additional importance.

During normal respiration, the pressure difference between inhalation and exhalation in the rear space of the nose is too low to transport odor molecules to the remote part of the olfactory mucosa. However, molecules diffuse effectively into the frontal sinus if high odor concentrations and a minimal inhalation time of two seconds are maintained.

Direction of the Track

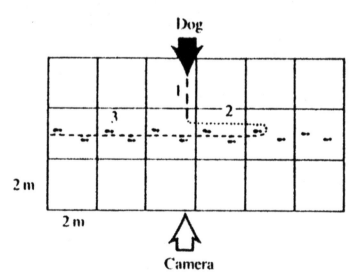

The dog's ability to determine the track direction was tested at a placement of footprints in the 2m x 2m grid. Only 18 of the 40 squares are shown. Here an example of one dog's way during the searching phase (1), the deciding phase (2) and the tracking phase (3).

In 1993, Aud Thesen and his team from the University of Oslo, Norway, studied the dog's ability to determine track direction. The ability to detect the direction of a track is of vital importance to animals of prey and is retained in many modern breeds of dogs. To study this ability, four trained German Shepherds were equipped with head microphones to transmit sniffing activity. In all tests the dogs were handled by their trainers. The test took place between noon and 3 P.M., throughout May to October in 1990 on an airfield near Oslo. The tests were carried out on a dry surface, on a dry, calm day with fair temperatures of 15 – 20° C. One week before the testing started, a grid of ten by four squares, each measuring two meters by two meters, was painted on the ground. All the dogs were video-monitored after being brought at right angles to a track where the position of each footprint was known. The trial began with the dog standing at heel about five meters from, and perpendicular to, the middle of the track. When given the order to track, the dog went straight forward, as they had been trained to do, while sniffing close to the ground. When it found the track, the dog turned either to the right or to the left.

In the dog's behavior, three phases could be recognized:

(1) an initial searching phase, during which the dog tried to find the track,
(2) a deciding phase, during which it tried to determine the direction of the track and
(3) a tracking phase, in which it followed the track.

During ten tests on twenty minute old tracks on grass, and ten tests on three minute old tracks on concrete, the dogs always followed the track in the correct direction. However, the dogs did not always turn in the correct direction when they first found the track. If the initial direction was wrong, the dogs turned abruptly and walked in the opposite direction. In the deciding phase the dogs moved at half speed and their periods of sniffing lasted three times as long as during the other two phases. Once the direction has been found they move faster, suggesting that following the track (the third phase) is a simpler task than determining its direction. Thus, the deciding phase seems to be the most difficult one; it is certainly the most impressive one from a human point of view. The dogs needed to smell in three to five seconds, only two to five footprints to decide in which direction the track had been laid, regardless whether it was on grass or concrete (other dogs under different conditions may require more prints).

It is assumed that the dogs determine the track direction by perceiving differences in the concentration of certain substances deposited by the tracklayer. This implies that, in some of the tests, the dogs must have determined a difference in the concentration of scent in the air above two consecutive prints which were made one second apart, either three minutes or twenty minutes earlier. To a human, this feat may appear unrealistic. The dog's ability to determine track direction in this time must rely on accurate methods of sampling air and the remarkable sensitivity for human odor substances. But Prof. Dr. W. Neuhaus had already written in 1953, that a dog's detection threshold for acetic acid, which is an important constituent of human skin secretions, may be a hundred million times lower than a human's threshold.

Chapter 5:
Fraud with Mantrailing

In the surrounding of Houston, Texas, a five-years-old girl was missing. After eight days her body was found in a wood area about ten kilometres from her home. It had been determined that before her death she had been violated and then strangled. In the vicinity, the police found some footprints and tracks of a car tire. A dog handler with his Bloodhound were asked for assistance...

The way in which a rope was tied around the child's neck immediately suspects a fifty four-years old man that already a year before was connected to the raping and strangling of a woman, but by lack of evidence was released.

At the crime scene, the Bloodhound was allowed to pick up the odor of the rope and the footprints. The dog tracked over the forest path and went in the direction of the city. After some kilometers, the handler decided that the already tired dog could come along with the police car. At each crossing the dog went out of the car and showed them the direction to drive. In that manner the company arrived at the house of the suspect, who of course denied any involvement in the matter.

K9 Fraud!

At the crime scene the Bloodhound was allowed to pick up the scent of the footprints

The dog tracked over the forest path and went in the direction of the city.

Chapter 5

Old Times Revive

The dog handler declared that his dog was trained as a 'mantrailer' and on an eight-days-old track, a Bloodhound can do it standing on his head.

In court, the suspect's lawyer examined the dog handler, who declared that his dog was trained as a 'mantrailer' and a Bloodhound can track an eight-day-old track while standing on it's head: 'Mantrailers can work out tracks of one and a half year or even older, and even follow the scent of someone transported in a car,' so the dog handler answered.

Those who have read the former chapters in this book, you remember the examples of about a century ago, of the times in which it was said that police dogs were able to perform remarkable, unbelievable and even impossible tracking results. Is this way of mantrailing a matter of fraud or is it realistic, and are dogs indeed able to put up such tremendous performances? Time to take a closer look at some remarkable cases!

The Jeffrey Allen Grant Case

During the late hours of September 18, 1998, Carolyn Ronlov in Belmont Shore near Long Beach, California was raped by a man she described as white with an ethnic accent. She was the seventh victim of rape in that town. From a scent pad created at the crime scene, the Bloodhound Tinkerbelle, of dog handler Dennis Slavin, an urban planner, attempted to track the assailant. She led the police from the Ronlov crime scene to a twenty unit apartment building about two miles away. The dog entered the building, went directly to the second floor, and then into the laundry room on that second floor. However, after ten minutes of attempting to pinpoint the scent, the dog became confused, and then gave up after failing to identify any particular unit or individual. Her handler inferred that it was because the building's poor ventilation that rendered any chance of an accurate track impossible. The dog did not show any interest in the apartment at any point throughout the evening. At the time, Jeffrey Allen Grant, a softball coach, lived in a unit on the first floor but he wasn't at home. Tinkerbelle did not show any interest in Grant's unit or in the first floor at any point. The officers sought to gather more information by questioning residents who were awakened by the commotion. Grant's apartment attracted the officers' attention first, because the lights were on in the apartment. When no one answered the door, the police marked him as a suspect. Two officers attempted to pick the locks on Grant's apartment door – with the intention of drawing the occupant outside. When the door did not open, the police testified that they grew even more suspicious and left with Grant as a possible suspect in their minds. Later, Tinkerbelle picked Grant from a crowd in a scent detection line-up at the Long Beach Police Department. Jeffrey Allen Grant was arrested as the Belmont Shore rapist and imprisoned. Only three months later he proved innocent by DNA tests; he had nothing to do with this case. And the real Belmont Shore rapist was caught in 2002 and lived in a totally different area!

Conclusion: A clear case of using an incompetent and uncertified dog and civilian dog handler, followed by wrong conclusions by the police. And after, with foreknowledge of who was the suspect, an absolutely inadmissible scent line-up was performed.

The Anthrax Letters

Just after the 9/11 attacks against the United States, on October 5, 2001 the residence of American were shocked again. Letters with the fatal bacterium Bacillus anthracis had been found in several people's mail. Five people were killed, at least seventeen others serious ill, mail delivery was paralyzed, and the anthrax-laced letters terrified the nation. Because the FBI after six months found no trace of a perpetrator, special agent Rex Stockham, an explosives expert of the FBI, who says he has no experience using

Following the track of a person in a moving vehicle has never been proven successful in a scientific test.

Bloodhounds himself, enlisted the help of three dog handlers from Southern California. Stockham said he first became acquainted with the three handlers after seeing a 1999 video of their experiments with taking scents from fragments of exploded bombs. These handlers were Bill Kift, a police officer in Long Beach, California, and his dog 'Lucy'; Dennis Slavin, the urban planner and meanwhile reserve officer with the South Pasadena Police Department, and 'Tinkerbelle' (who before the aforesaid case Grant had failed); and Ted Hamm, a civilian who runs his own Bloodhound business and is used by the Los Angeles County Sheriff's Department, and 'Knight'.

These handlers extracted scent samples from an evidence with the use of a machine called the Scent Transfer Unit (STU-100). Originally invented by Bill Tolhurst, and further refined and marketed by Larry Harris, the machine that resembles a small vacuum cleaner is designed to draw the scent off the article and deposit it on a sterile gauze pad. This controversial device is criticised because an older scent might linger in the machine when it is used on a new case, in that way contaminate scents and bring false positives that could botch criminal cases. Gilbert Levy, a defense attorney, later in this chapter discussed the Joshua Wade case, wrote in court filings that the STU-100 method has been proven to be unreliable. 'It is not accepted by many in the dog handling law enforcement community,' including the Law Enforcement Bloodhound Association and the National Police Bloodhound Association. At least two Californian homicide convictions based on dog evidence gathered by the STU-100 was used, were later overturned.

From two anthrax-tainted letters, that way scent pads were lifted; however, this took place half a year after those letters went through the postal system, rubbing against other letters with other scents, and after finding the letters which were anthrax laced they were decontaminated using radiation, which might affect the scent. And finally, the letters went through lots of hands for investigation.

In the mean time, scientists in the close-knit biowarfare community began suggesting that a disgruntled ex-employee at Fort Detrick, the nation's premier biodefense lab, was the most likely perpetrator. The press pounced on Dr. Steven J. Hatfill, who once worked at Fort Detrick, and also the FBI became interested in this man. According to Mark Miller and Daniel Klaidman in August 2002:

Chapter 5

'Early last week FBI agents, on the trail of last year's anthrax attacker, turned to a 16th-century technology to help solve a 21th-century crime. Agents presented the canines with 'scent packs' lifted from anthrax-tainted letters (long since decontaminated) in hopes that some faint, telltale trace of the perpetrator's smell still remained months after the fact. The agents quietly brought the dogs to various locations frequented by a dozen people they considered possible suspects – hoping the hounds would match the scent on the letters. In place after place the dogs had no reaction. But when the handlers approached the Frederick Md. apartment building of Dr. Steven J. Hatfill, an eccentric forty eight-year-old scientist who had worked in one of the Army's top bioweapons-research laboratories, the dogs immediately became agitated. NewsWeek proclaimed: 'They went crazy,' says one law-enforcement source. The agents also brought the Bloodhounds to the Washington, D.C., apartment of Hartfill's girlfriend and to a Denny's restaurant in Louisiana, where Hatfill had eaten the day before. In both places the dogs jumped and barked, indicating they'd picked up the scent.'

As a result of this information, Dr. Hatfill was arrested and a search warrant was issued for his apartment, but the investigation netted no direct evidence against Dr. Hatfill, and he was set free. Dr. Hatfill adamantly denied having anything to do with the anthrax attacks, saying he has been targeted by investigators desperate showing no progress in the year-old case.

July 27, 2008 Bruce Edwards Ivins, a former collegue of Dr. Hatfill, who worked for eighteen years in the Fort Detrick laboratories, committed suicide prior to formal charges being filed by the FBI in link to the anthrax letters of 2001. August 6, 2008, the FBI and the United States Department of Justice formally announced that 'the Government had concluded that Ivins was likely to have been solely responsible for the deaths of five persons, and the injury of dozens of others, resulting from the mailing of several anonymous letters to members of Congress and members of the media in September and October, 2001. These letters contained Bacillus anthracis, commonly referred to as anthrax.'

Conclusion: Again use of uncertified dogs, of which one earlier had failed in a major case. Furthermore the use of letters, which were cross contaminated with other human scents, and an unvalidated method and machine to transfer scent to gauze pads. Then foreknowledge of a suspect due to the press indicated name of Dr. Hatfill, and the false alerts of the dogs. After which Dr. Hatfill's reputation and life were completely destroyed.

The Scott Peterson Case

'She stared out at the water, facing the direction of the wind, turned around and gave me the 'end of trail' indication.'

On December 24, 2002, the eight months pregnant Laci Peterson was reported missing from her home in Modesto, California. Soon her husband Scott Peterson was suspected of being involved in her disappearance. Four days after she was reported missing, dogs and civilian dog handlers of the California Rescue Dog Association (CARDA) went out searching. To get Laci's scent the dogs got odor from a pair of sunglasses taken from the Petersons' house. Before they began, no one asked if any other people, including Scott had touched the sunglasses.

Dog handler Cindee Valentin and her Bloodhound 'Merlin' took the scent from the pair of sunglasses, after which the dog tracked from the couple's Modesto home many miles through the city to the intersection of Highway 132, which leads to San Francisco Bay, the place Scott had told to be fishing at the day of Laci's disappearance. The dog handler said she'd learned enough to know that Laci was taken away from her home in a vehicle. She explained that on the day of tracking, her dog never sniffed sidewalks: 'It only followed Laci's scent on a direct track right down the middle of streets' and Valentin told the detectives that 'a trained tracking dog following a scent down the middle of the street is a sure indication a person was in a vehicle...'

Near the bay Eloise Anderson, a member of the Contra Costa Search and Rescue Team and handler of a trailing dog named 'Trimble' went on searching. Trimble was brought to the area where Scott said he launched his boat to go fishing, and there she gave her Labrador Retriever the scent from Laci's sunglasses. 'The dog grew excited. She pulled hard on the leash, taking me out to a pier where she stopped and stared out at the water. Then she turned around and gave me an indication that the trail had ended. I stood for a minute to see if she would move on or stick to the end of trail indication. Trimble then gave a 'hard end of trail indication' indicating that Laci was out there somewhere,' the dog handler explained in court.

Conclusion: Again a case of using incompetent, and for police work, uncertified dogs and civilian dog handlers. Also, using a pair of sunglasses that could have also be handled by her husband or others as a 'scent article' to start the dog looking for a trail is a big mistake. Then the foreknowledge about the way Scott Peterson drove to his fishing spot near the bay, and after that declare on oath that the dog followed that track all by himself, many miles and at the middle of a paved road. Following the track of a person in a moving car is impossible, and has never been proven in a scientific test. And about the interpretation of the dog handler, that her dog gave her the 'end of trail' indication, we don't have to talk. All of this considering, 'end of the line' best describes this forensic investigation.

Stupid Utterances

Civilians are not the only ones who say stupid things about dogs. In September 2002, the Bloodhounds Lucy, Tinkerbelle and Knight and their dog handlers were in Baton Rouge, the capital city of Louisiana, in order to help the FBI find a serial killer.

Rex Stockham, in a press meeting quoted Steve Ritea saying: 'that the dogs have been known to pick up a scent up to three years old, and that scents can come from something as small as a shell casing fired from a gun,'

Dennis Slavin, the dog handler of Tinkerbelle, said the dogs are also capable of picking out a persons' scent from an object even after it has been handled

'Dogs have been known to pick up scents up to three years old. The scent can come from something as small as a shell casing fired from a gun.'

by dozens – perhaps hundreds – of other people. To demonstrate, Ted Hamm, the dog handler of Knight, asked four reporters to touch a sheet of paper and then used the STU-100 to transfer their scents to a sterile gauze pad. Three of the reporters were asked to stand side by side as a fourth ran around a corner about two hundred and fifty feet away while the dog sniffed all four scents on the pad. After smelling the three reporters in plain sight, the dog then took off around the corner, let out a howl and ran to the fourth reporter, who was sitting quietly on a low wall.

And in order to worsen this bad joke, Slavin said: 'The dogs have performed the same demonstration to find a single person out of forty eight others!'

Dog Handler Sandra Anderson

According to Daniel A. Smith, the best example of law enforcement agencies (local, state, and federal) using dog handler to assist in criminal investigations without proper and sufficient qualifications is Sandra Anderson of Midland, Michigan. Her mixed Doberman named Eagle was believed by law enforcement agencies around the world as the best cadaver search dog there ever was. Anderson was used extensively by the FBI to search for body parts in high profile cases. Eventhough it was said that the FBI was warned a number of times that Anderson was a fraud and her dog couldn't do what she claimed.

Daniel Smith continues: In April 2002, a law enforcement officer saw Anderson remove a bone from her boot during a search in Oscoda, Michigan, and throw it on the ground. Anderson than claimed Eagle found another bone. This

Chapter 5

All dog handlers in forensic investigations require accreditation, and must perform according to an identified protocol.

lead to an excessive investigation of Anderson and concluded with a ten count indictment in August 2003. Anderson was charged with evidence tampering, obstruction of justice, and lying to investigators. The charges said she not only planted bones in the search area, but that she also used her own body fluids to stain a hack saw blade, money and pieces of cloth. There are a great number of cases Anderson was involved in that had to undergo appeals.

Dog Handler Penny Bell

Penny Bell, of Milwaukee Wisconson, is another current dog handler who law enforcement casts a doubt on. She claims her Bloodhound Hoover Von Vacuum can track a human scent of more than two months old. Alleged, her dog can even correctly worked out a two years old track, and she has claimed responsibility for several successful searches. Bell said, Hoover found a body in the Menomonee River in Milwaukee in a 1998 case. According John A. Zautke, a battalion chief with the Milwaukee Fire Department, Bell didn't find the body and wasn't even in the neighbourhood when the body was recovered. 'Not even close,' he said. 'She said the dog pinpointed it. This dog stopped every ten feet along and drank some water. We have some real good search teams here, and they didn't want anything to do with her.'

In 2003, after seeing at a television report of a cold case of two missing boys, Penny Bell contacted the parents and went with her dog on search two months after their disappearance. Bell said her dog tracked a scent to a westbound entrance ramp to Interstate 94 in Minneapolis.

John A. Zautke had instructed police to keep her away from search scenes, where she shows up uninvited and contaminates search sites. Detective Dave Hoeschen of the Stearns County Sheriff's Office said he watched her with the dog on one of the searches and said he has no confidence in her work. He said she occasionally pulled the dog in the direction she wanted it to go rather than letting the dog lead. Hoover has no accreditation. Most states, including Minnesota, don't require accreditation.

Police dog expert Terry Shoenbach, quoted in Daniel A. Smith's book, stated he is familiar with Bell and her dog. He stated there are a lot of controversies surrounding her claims. Shoenbach says that there is no way she can do what she claims. 'This case is very similar to all the other frauds running around from scene to scene making outrageous claims of finds. This case is very similar to John Preston, Sandra Anderson and the dogs and handlers involved in the Scott Peterson case. These people are not certified by any legitimate canine associates, their claims are unsubstantiated, all they want to see is their name in the paper and in my opinion are downright liars.'

Chapter 5

Dog Handler Keith Pikett (1)

In the late evening of March 15, 2006, the strangled body of the Sally Blackwell, a fifty three-year-old Texas Child Protective Services worker, was found in her nightgown in a field off Hanselman Road near the city of Victoria, about five miles from her home. After determining the body had been transported there, the Victoria Police Department brought in a team of Bloodhounds from the Texas Department of Criminal Justice to search for evidence and attempt to follow the trail. The dogs quickly lost the trail where the field met the road.

Deputy Keith Pikett, from the Fort Bend County

The strangled body was found in a field about five miles from her home.

Sheriff's office, and his team of Bloodhounds who have been used statewide to track crime suspects from homicide scenes, were then brought in to pick up the scent. One of his Bloodhounds, Quincy, started tracking a scent taken from her body to the Cimarron neighborhood where Sally Blackwell lived. About two miles into the trail, Pickett switched dogs. 'It's kind of a check, to see if the first dog made a mistake – you can confirm by seeing if the second dog picks up the trail,' he said. That Bloodhound, James Bond, was given the scent and he led officers first to Sally Blackwell's house and then to former Victoria County

Sheriff's Capt. Michael Buchanek's house nearby. Capt. Buchanek, who had briefly dated Blackwell, was already under suspicion by some members of the police department.

Two separate scent line-ups were conducted. The dogs were given the homicide scene scent again and through verbal and hand cues, asked to select its match with scents taken from six white males. The dogs selected Buchanek's scent both times. 'The dogs are rarely wrong,' Pikett said. Four months later it was clear that the DNA found under Sally's fingernails belonged to a twenty five-year-old Victoria man, Jeffrey Grimsinger, who pleaded guilty to kidnapping and killing the woman. Grimsinger is serving life in prison.

Conclusion: The police already suspected Capt. Michael Buchanek because of a broken relation, and their theory was that he transported the body of Sally in the trunk of his car to the field. The dogs therefore tracked the scent of the victim in the car twenty four hours after it was created – from the field more than five miles over the road, back to her house, and after that to Capt. Buchanek's house. An exceptional performance that no dog can copy, not mentioning the influencing with verbal and hand cues during the scent line-up. Keith Pikett has been sued in federal court for fraud involving his dogs.

Dog Handler Keith Pikett (2)

That his dogs are rarely wrong was also a lie of Keith Pikett, because for the second time in less than a year he had been sued in federal court for fraud involving his dogs. A complete special report about Pikett's 'highly dubious dog work' was published by the Innocence Project of Texas with the title *'Dog Scent Lineups, A Junk Science Injustice'* in September 2009.

Quoting Rick Casey in February, 2009, Calvin Lee Miller, a self-employed mechanic and laborer, was called into the Yoakum Police Department for questioning. He took his attorney, Bill Caraway, with him. According to a lawsuit on Miller's behalf, a police officer grabbed Miller's arm, wiped it 'forcibly' with a gauze pad, and said, 'That's all I need. Y'all can go now.' The police version is less aggressive, but it is undisputed that the purpose of the encounter was to obtain skin cells that contained Miller's scent so that one of Fort Bend County

Deputy Keith Pikett's Bloodhounds could check his scent against scents found on evidence connected with two crimes.

According to the suit, police told Caraway that 'local dope dealers' said Miller had been buying a lot of cocaine and a local woman, sixty six-years-old, had reported being robbed by a tall, soft-spoken black man – a description that fits Miller and quite a few other black males. A few weeks later, a seventy nine-year-old Yoakum woman was raped, also describing her assailant as a tall, soft-spoken black man.

Miller was jailed March 4, based partly on a 'scent line-up' conducted by Pikett in which he had his Bloodhound compare Miller's scent to scents found on the rape victim's bedcover and items recovered from the robbery. A DNA test excluded Miller as the rapist in early April, but he wasn't released for more than a month, four days after both victims failed to identify him in a line-up.

Conclusion: Quoting the Innocence Project of Texas in 2009, Pikett testified under oath that his dog Clue, only once erred in 1 659 scent identifications, and James Bond had been wrong once out of 2 266 line-ups. A fourth Bloodhound, twelve-year-old Quincy, performed 2 831 scent line-ups and made only three mistakes early in her career. According to the research done by the Dutch police (Schoon & Haak) this is absolutely impossible. Or like Daniel Smith wrote in his book: 'If it sounds too good to be true – it probably is!'

What is Mantrailing?

In principle, we know three kinds of methods in search dogs for human odor: tracking (with the dog's nose close to the ground), air scenting (with higher held nose, the dog tries to find wind-blown human odor) and mantrailing (searching for the indivudal odor trail of a person after smelling a 'scent article'.) In mantrailing, it is up to the dog to follow the trail close to the prints, depending on weather conditions, terrain circumstances and preferences of the dog.

In principle mantrailing can be done by every dog breed, but most of the time dog handlers prefer to work with Bloodhounds. This is because it is said that Bloodhounds 'can follow a track in every terrain, also in towns, and days after and in extreme cases, even after weeks. Because the dog follows a certain individual human odor, he has no problems to do that in areas strongly contaminated by other odors.'

According to the American Bloodhound Club in certifications we distinguish a Mantrailer (MT) with a trail that is approximately one-half a mile (880 yards,) and no more than three-quarters mile (1320 yards.) MT trails will be at least four hours old but no more than six hours old and will include one change of direction in the form of a turn or curve that is no less than 90º.

The Mantrailer Intermediate-level (MTI) is a trail that is approximately one-half mile (880 yards) long and no more than three-quarters mile (1320 yards) long. Trails will be run in an area of moderate contamination (school yard, parking area, etc.) that has moderate access during all phases of the test. MTI trails will be at least eight hours old but no more than eighteen hours old and will follow a 'natural wandering

'Because it is a Bloodhound' doesn't automatically mean they can track or trail. Also Bloodhounds have to be trained carefully.

path,' including two changes of direction, one of which must be a turn of at least 90 degrees.

The Mantrailer Excellent-level (MTX) is a trail that is approximately one-half mile (880 yards) long and no more than three-quarters mile (1320 yards) long. Trails will be run in a heavily contaminated area (mall, school yard, public park, forest, industrial area or similar heavily used area) that has unlimited access and heavy traffic during all phases of the test. MTX trails will be at least twenty-four hours old but no more than thirty-six hours old and will follow a 'natural wandering path,' including two changes of direction, one of which must be a turn of at least 90 degrees. MTX trails will also include no more than three obstacles consisting of roads, a water crossing (water that can be walked through), a bridge, cross tracks, a contaminated area with another person in it, or a terrain change.

Trailing is a test of a dog's ability to distinguish and follow one person's scent and identify that person. Judges will give handlers their scent articles when they conduct trail briefings. The specific scent article choice will be a sterile gauze pad or a sheet of clean cotton cloth, 4' x 4', worn by the runner, next to the skin, for at least one hour. Scent articles may be carried by exhibitors or left at the starting stake. Exhibitors may re-scent their dogs at any time along the trail at their discretion. Cross runners are used on the MTI and MTX trails, and the runners are located at the end of the trail. The dog must identify the correct runner. A trailing dog can air scent, ground scent or use any other means to get from point 'A' to point 'B' the quickest and most efficient way possible.

Jerry Nichols, president of the Law Enforcement Bloodhound Association, headquartered in Denver, when asked about following a seven-week-old scent, he said, 'I don't know any dog – any credible dog – that can do this. The best chance is within the first forty eight hours. After that, chances greatly diminish because of time, and the elements.'

What Can't Mantrailers Do?

For a start, mantrailers cannot perform the unbelievable achievements more times claimed, but never proved in scientific tests! This concerns Bloodhounds as all other breeds or cross-breeds.

- Mantrailers cannot follow tracks or trails better than all other well-trained search dogs.

- Mantrailers are not always able to find the track or trail belonging to the scent article at the beginning.

- Mantrailers cannot follow tracks or trails of several days old on paved roads in towns.

- Mantrailers cannot follow tracks or trails of a person transported in a car.

Mantrailers cannot follow tracks or trails better than all other well-trained search dogs...

Chapter 5

The Scent Article Method Project

In a scientific test in 2001 no dog could fulfil the requirements
and the SAM-project was stopped...

In England, 1998, a three-year project conducted by Essex police and funded by the Home Office, started to test the efficiency of the mantrailing method. Bloodhound 'Sherlock' and another Bloodhound named 'Morse' – like the television detective – alongside two German Shepherd Dogs, 'Scully' and 'Reagan', were enlisted as puppies to be trained in SAM, the 'scent article method' of sniffing out suspects.

Despite some early successes, the experiment did not work out. In a scientific test in 2001, no dog could fulfil the requirements and the project was stopped. At that time the tested Bloodhounds and hunting dogs at police dog schools in Bavaria (Germany) and Vienna (Austria) also fell short of expectations.

As a result of the SAM-test in Essex, the Dutch police decided not to start a training program with Bloodhounds and/or mantrailers.

Bloodhounds – Tracking or Trailing

We will not dispute that Bloodhounds can track or trail. Well trained Bloodhounds with the right temperament and drives can track or trail as well as every other dog breed. A disadvantage of Bloodhounds can be that they are sometimes stubborn and rather tough if they don't want to work, or do not see the point of it. 'Because it is a Bloodhound' doesn't mean it automatically can track or trail. Also, Bloodhounds have to be trained carefully, which by beginners often is underestimated.

Fraud suspected Penny Bell claimed that 'basically, Bloodhounds don't need any training – it is a natural instinct.' Bell said she trained Hoover herself after attending about a week of seminars some years ago. She said she's also learned from television shows, including 'CSI: Crime Scene Investigation.' Hoover has no accreditation. To defend this, Bell replied 'I believe Bloodhounds should not be certified... Why should I be teaching my dog something that it does naturally?'

Five Big Mistakes in Mantrailing

In mantrailing there are five main causes of faults.

• First of all, the incorrect assumption that individual human odor substances, such as flakes of skin or odor molecules, glide for a very long time in the air, and by this can be smelled by dogs for very long time. This is based on an unproven theory of Dr. R.J. Clifford, later also published by W.G. Syrotuck.

According to this theory, there are about two billion cells composing the human skin, of which about 1/30 are released daily as dead flakes of skin. This would mean that, per minute, more than forty thousand cells fall from our body. On this information, they based their theory that trailing dogs follow this 'flakes of skin track'. Also, these flakes of skin, by the wind, are blown and pile up at certain spots in terrains or at sides of buildings, etc.

The followers of this theory dare to claim that those flakes of skin will remain in their certain spots, never to be blown again by the wind, or traffic, and remain so for week, perhaps months!

Arguments against this theory is the comprehensive research of police officer Major Konrad Most, as discussed in the former chapter. In which he used a cable-lift to pull a person on a floating apparatus above the ground. All well trained dogs stopped tracking at the point where the test person became elevated above the ground. It's for sure, Konrad Most concluded, that human odor substances falling from above do not produce enough of a track for the dog to follow. Based on this research of Konrad Most and his floating apparatus, and on our own experiments, we believe that this 'flakes of skin' theory doesn't hold water.

- A second important cause of faults are the so-called 'Clever Hans' cues, discussed in Chapter 2. The importance of the 'cue experiments' is that they illustrate how well dogs can learn to 'read' us. During training, we want the dogs to respond to the relevant cue. So, when searching for human odor, the only cue must be odor. Observing trainers and handlers with their dogs, sometimes a cue is obvious. A minimal movement of the instructor is enough for a dog to respond. But how can we prevent ourselves from cueing the dog in some way, if they can pick up such minimal signals? The answer is obvious: work 'blind', which means do not know the direction or the end of the track, and preferably have no one close by who knows it since this person may also unconsciously cue the dog.

- A third fault which often happens is contamination of the scent article. In the Netherlands, a special protocol makes clear in what way the initial scent sample at the crime scene – the corpus delicti – has to be collected and how it has to be preserved and stored. That protocol is based on years of methodical observation and scientific research (Schoon & Haak). The first officers on the scene of the crime must be aware of the possibility of scent identifications right from the beginning. This prevents the contamination of relevant material. For example, a window may have been opened by a burglar using a crowbar. The crowbar may be very rough, making it impossible to lift fingerprints off it.

The method of storing materials necessary for scent identification line-up training. (KLPD, 2002.)

However, it will certainly contain the odor of a perpetrator who brought the crowbar with him, and used it to force the window. The officer arriving on the crime scene must be aware of this and not to touch the crowbar himself. Even if this officer is unaware of scent identification line-ups, the crowbar will certainly be taken as a piece of evidence and attempts will be made to match the marks found in the window frame to the crowbar. When collecting a crowbar for this purpose, there is no harm in touching it. But when collecting the crowbar for scent identification or DNA test purposes, the scent traces on it need to be left intact and not mixed with more scent traces.

So, even the first officer on the crime scene has to be aware of the possibilities of scent identification line-ups. In short, the selection of the item to collect or to take a scent sample from has to be done in an intelligent way. Ideally, objects that are linked to the crime itself are selected. The general rules of selection are: objects that have been brought to the crime scene by the perpetrator are best,

Chapter 5

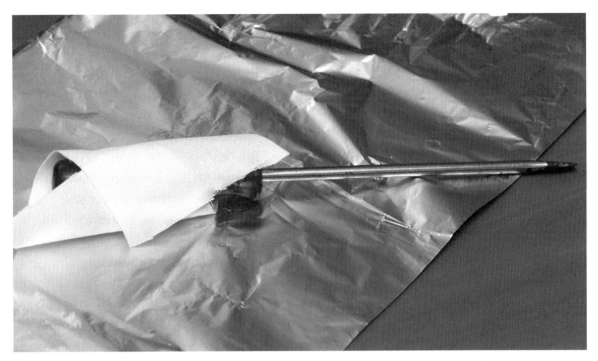

The Dutch Police method of collecting scent samples from the scene of a crime. (KLPD, 2002.)

objects found on the scene of the crime that have certainly been touched by the perpetrator are also good. Wet or dirty objects, or objects that several people have touched, or objects that have been lying outside for a couple of days are less desirable but cannot not excluded, especially if they are significant to the case.

With the advance of science, objects that are collected at a crime scene are examined in many different ways. The sequence of these examinations has become a point of interest. For example: rubbing an object with a cotton absorber for scent sample collection will certainly destroy any fingerprints. It is better not to rub the object if fingerprints are to be collected, but to drape the cotton absorber loosely over the object. Combining scent sample collection with DNA analysis is another point where conflict may arise. This is under investigation. These two examples demonstrate the necessity of having scent trace collection integrated into the normal working procedures. This must be done in conjunction with other institutes such as forensic laboratories.

To obtain good scent traces, it is imperative that officers at the crime scene not only know which objects to select, but also how to collect them. It is clear that small mistakes in the beginning can have significant consequences later on in the investigation. After deciding on the relevant objects, the scents have to be collected and preserved. If the objects are relatively small and can be preserved as a whole, this can be done by putting them in a thick plastic bag and tying it with a knot, expelling as much air as possible out of the bag beforehand. Another preservation method is putting the object into a clean glass jar with a twist-off top. If the object is big and unwieldy, or if it cannot be removed (a car seat for example), or if the object needs to be used for other purposes, a scent sample can be made. A piece of cotton absorber is placed over the object, and this is usually covered with aluminum foil and pressed down to maximize the contact between the object and the cotton absorber. This is left for at least 30 minutes and then removed. The cotton absorber is put into a glass jar with a twist-off top. Scent traces are usually stored in rooms with little or no daylight and a relatively constant room temperature. Sunlight is especially detrimental to odor, so this needs to be avoided. A room with limited access and a proper registration of incoming and outgoing articles is recommended.

A final prerequisite for a proper collection of scent traces is to organize the logistics well. Officers collecting scent traces should have the correct material available: the right kind of plastic bags, tweezers, glass jars, scent absorbers, aluminum foil, sealing material etc. This will prevent objects from being collected in paper bags and such.

- The fourth important cause of faults is the quality of the odor at the corpus delicti or the scent article. For instance: A fingerprint expert first analyses the quality of the fingerprint on an object. He can say, beforehand, that the quality of the fingerprint is insufficient for him to be able to make comparisons. This means that a fingerprint expert simply cannot work with poor-quality fingerprints, only trying to make matches based on good starting material. Unfortunately, there is no similar method to measure the quality of the odor left on an object. From experiments it is known that dogs can detect human odor on objects, even left outside, for days and sometimes weeks. However, this does not mean that the quality of this odor, or the fullness of the scent picture, is sufficient to be able to identify this person. In this way, odor resembles memory that is vital in eyewitness confrontations. There is no way to measure the quality of a memory someone has of an incident this person has witnessed. Even so, eyewitnesses of crimes are confronted with line-ups of people and are asked to identify anyone they recognize from the incident. And as we all know, memories can be very incorrect.

We also have to be aware that scent traces can only be used once. When they are taken out of their packaging and breathed upon by a dog, the odor starts to change. Repackaging the material can be considered, but one has to accept that the odor on the object or the scent sample has changed significantly.

• The fifth, and just as important fault: Some dog handlers want personal gain and will attempt to achieve it any way possible. Proving their dog can do something special, by eventually leading the dog in a certain and fraudulent direction.

The Joshua Wade Case

August 3, 2007, Mindy Schloss, a fifty two-years-old psychiatric nurse from Anchorage, Alaska vanished. Six days later her car was found in a parking lot near the airport. On the steering wheel DNA was found of her neighbor Joshua Wade, twenty seven, who in 2003, was acquitted of murdering Della Brown, thirty three, in a Spenard shack. In 2000, he was arrested on felony charges of robbery and burglary, which were later reduced. He has a history of smaller crimes and domestic violence.

In the beginning Joshua Wade was arrested and charged in federal court with bank fraud for using Mindy Schloss' ATM card on August 5 and 6. He stole $1 000, before an ATM machine withheld the stolen card. But when six weeks later on September 13, her somewhat decomposed body was found partially burned and shot to death in the woods off Knik-Goose Bay Road in Wasilla – Wade was charged with the murder.

In this case, the investigators, roughly two weeks after Mandy Schloss

The Bloodhounds followed the 12 day old track for over 4 miles in an urban environment. From two ATMs in the center of the city - a place frequented by heavy pedisterian traffic.

went missing, flew in Bloodhounds and their handlers to Alaska. These were Dennis Slavin with Tinkerbelle and Bill Kift with Lucy, both the handlers that drastically failed in the Jeffrey Grant Case from 1998, and the Anthrax Letters in 2001 with the misdirected investigation of Dr. Steven Hatfill. Also the controversial STU-100 machine was used again.

In several cases, scent samples were collected from items of evidence that had not been sufficiently protected (such as the seat of Mandy's car after numerous people had been in the car) and law enforcement failed to exclude all known persons who could have contributed to the scent sample at the beginning of some of the searches.

The tracks in this case were over twelve days old, in an urban environment and some were several miles long. The Bloodhounds followed the scents taken from Mandy's abandoned car and from two ATMs, where investigators say Wade used her card after her disappearance. One trail stretched over four miles and ended directly at the side door of Wade's house. The dogs also followed his scent from the corner of Cutty Sark Street, where Wade and Schloss both lived, to Schloss's car, which was abandoned near the airport.

The dog handlers also testified they'd used their dogs to rule out involvement

Chapter 5

Do you think a dog, even a trained Bloodhound, can really pick up a scent and track a man over four miles across a town weeks after he made the trip?

by other people in Wade's house. They did this by taking samples of their scents to the site where Schloss' body was recovered in the wooded area in Wasilla. They claimed 'that the FBI Bloodhounds have been trained not to move when given a scent pad if the scent isn't present at a scene. More than two months after Mandy's body was found, at the crime scene, the only scent pad that got a response came from Wade.

In court, Rex Stockham the supervisor of the FBI's human scent evidence team, who works with the dogs that tracked Wade explained 'that the dogs are trained to pick up human scent trails made of odor and sluffed skin cells. They can find trails made by people in cars because the car ventilation system blows out odors. They can also pick up trails of people traveling by bike,' he said. 'Human scent dogs are different than tracking dogs used to find criminals on the run. Those track from footprint to footprint. They're also different than dogs used to find bombs, blood or cadavers. Those dogs are trained to find a specific smell. A body scent trail is more diffused than footprints. It's like dust that settles on surfaces along a trail. The wind can disturb it, pushing it against walls and into cracks, while humidity makes it stick,' Stockham explained. 'The trails can last weeks or even months, though they diminish over time. Dogs can also detect specific scents on surfaces that have been submerged in water . . .'

'Human scent trails are viable for days, weeks and sometimes months,' said Dennis Slavin, the handler of Tinkerbelle. 'Human scent will be caught up against the edges of buildings, curb lines ... and will adhere to things in its path.'

Conclusion: After reading this far into the book: do you think a dog, even a trained Bloodhound, can really pick up a scent and track a man over four miles across town, weeks after he made the trip – some of it on a bicycle? And can a dog correctly trail a suspect in an automobile? In a prison in Anchorage Joshua Wade faces the death penalty because of absolutely malafide and impermissable dog search investigation . . .

Chapter 6:
Human Odor and Dog's Scent Perception

There are a lot of things that influence the achievements of the tracking or trailing dog. There are soil damages, often caused by kicking or shuffling and walking over the ground causes physical changes that bring out specific scents of plants or soils. Furthermore scents of footwear, like the original scent of shoes or boots, shoe polish, as well as items ground into the soles and, of course, the individual human odor which is also very important in other search work like scent identification line-up.

Scents of the Track

THE SCENT COMPLEX of a track consists, beside of individual human odor, of soil damage from physical changes and specific scents of plants. When a tracklayer walks over a meadow, there are several changes made by his footprints. First, there are some physical changes. The weight of the human body creates pressure on the ground. The print of the footwear will press down a little into the ground, depending on the weight of the tracklayer and the composition of the soil. On ploughed land the footprint can be clearly recognized, and it causes visible damage to the ground's surface. Because of this change to the ground, humidity and biological odors are set free from the Earth. Bacteria from greenery breaking down leaves humus, which gives a certain scent to the soil. The pressure of footsteps causes this scent to appear, and we smell about the same as when we weed our gardens.

A footstep, however, will cause more physical changes to the overgrowth.

When a tracklayer walks over a meadow, there are several changes made by his footprints, like bent or broken-off parts of plants, grass, weeds and twigs.

There will be visible changes, like bent or broken off parts of plants, like grasses, weeds and twigs. And there will be invisible changes, damaged or killed insects and micro-organisms. Further, the pressure of the human body and the friction as we walk on the ground causes a small amount of heat.

Just as every soil has its own characteristic scent, plants, weeds, grasses and flowers have their own specific scent. Damaging parts of the plant sets free a strong scent of plant sap and these have an important influence on the scent of the track. Everyone who has taken leaf off a geranium knows what is meant by setting free a scent after damaging a plant. A just-mowed lawn also has such a specific scent. Humans need large amounts of scent before they can perceive it, but for dogs the damage caused by one footstep is already more than enough to smell the plant sap. The scents that exist after plants and grasses are damaged are, just like soil, almost immediately set free and smellable. The intensity of this scent increases very quickly, but these scents disappear rather quickly as well.

The weight of the human body creates pressure on the ground. The print of the footwear will press down a little, depending on the weight of the tracklayer and the composition of the soil.

The flow of the plant saps stop after a certain period of time, because the plants and the Earth work hard on the recovery of the damage. That recovery is caused by all sorts of micro-organism in and on the plants and soil. The wounds in the plants and grasses will close fast, just like a wound in our skin, and the dead or dying-off parts of the plants are cleared away by bacteria that make things rot. Then another change takes place. The scent caused by these bacteria will, after a certain period of time, turn into a stench, which is a clear smell for dogs. It is like a dung heap or the odor of a haystack. Anyone who has ever smelled a pile of grass after one rainy day knows what kind of scent these rotting bacteria cause. The scent of broken twigs comes about in the same way as grass and plants. The damaged or killed insects and other small animals, of course, leave their own specific scents on the track. For the rotting bacteria to work at its optimal level, a certain amount of humidity and warmth is necessary. A part of that warmth is caused by the pressure of our feet on the soil and the friction of walking. With that, the humidity also comes out of the ground. So these are the optimal circumstances for the bacteria to start their work of clear off damage. But when this little bit of warmth and humidity are used up, more has to be withdrawn from the surroundings.

How far the work of the bacteria can be continued depends on the outside temperature and the relative humidity of the environment. A very high

Rubber, leather and all the materials used for footwear each have their unique scent.

temperature will decrease the reproduction of the bacteria, which delays their action. The same happens at extreme low temperatures. Furthermore, dry air is more a disadvantage for the life of bacteria than humid air. Because the bacteria also play an important role in human odors, we can partly determine the ideal weather conditions for tracking. For an efficient microbe, and optimal scent creation by these bacteria, the humidity of the air has to be average to high, and the temperature should be neither too high nor too low. That means temperatures around 20 º C, measured at about one and a half meters above ground.

Any type of footwear can be worn by a tracklayer. Of course, rubber, leather and all the materials used for footwear each have their specific scent, which together form the specific scent of the footwear. The added scents of the chemical finishes, such as protective coatings and polishes also contribute to the scent of footwear. Normal walking will wear off small bits of the soles, especially on a hard surface, and these are left on the track; these parts also contribute to the scent complex of the track. There are all sorts of things that are left under the soles that contribute to the scent complex – everything we tread in. These may be pleasant scents for the dog, or they could be very repulsive scents, and that makes it more difficult to track. During tracking we have to take into account that as the terrain changes, or the soil, some of the last terrain walked on will always be carried under the footwear. This will be brought onto the first few feet of the next terrain to be walked on. For instance, coming from a meadow onto a road, some odors of plants will be carried under the soles and left on the beginning of that road.

Human Odor in the Track

It is still believed by some trainers that in tracking the individual odor of the tracklayer, their odor plays no particular role. According to them, other factors determine the track in a certain way. In their opinion, the odor of the tracklayer exists in such a small quantity on the track that, even when this odor is present, it should disappear under the other scent components. On the other hand, others believe the individual human odor is what dogs search for. Only that way can a well-trained dog stay on track, even over hard road surfaces, and not be diverted by cross-tracks made around the same time.

After reading these two opinions, one can ask: Is it or is it not possible for the dog to perceive the human odor component in a track? To determine whether a dog could successfully do this Dr. Walter Neuhaus in 1953 calculated human sweat production and sweat odors. These he compared with the dog's very low threshold values for odors, which he determined in earlier experiments. He concluded that the amount of human odor in normal tracks, even after hours, was

While searching for an individuals odor, this Dutch police dog stays on track, even over hard paved surfaces.

enough to be perceived by the dog. This conclusion was based on the threshold values for separate, clear odor substances. But human odor is a mixture of odors. As a follow up, three years later, Dr. Neuhaus investigated the prickle of equal receptors by multiple odor substances, and found lower threshold values for such mixtures. His earlier conclusion that dogs could perceive human odor was therefore strengthened. Even if an odor was surrounded by another strong scent, the dog could observe even minor deviations in the odor mix. This agrees with the observation that a dog can recognize the odor of a human, and an article touched by that human, even when this article has a stronger scent itself, or has another strong scent on it.

This situation can occur while a dog is on track – as can other changes of scents, like shifting from a meadow into a wood – which plays a big role. Even when the other scent components of the track are about a thousand times stronger than the human odor, it is still possible for the dog to recognize the individual human odor in the track (Gerritsen and Haak, 2001).

Scents of the Trail

All mammals produce a number of different odors. Expiration of air, urine, feces, exocrine glandular secretions, and body openings all contain odorous substances. For our purposes, we will focus on the odor of the skin. In general, this is thought to be the sum of genetic differences, bacterial action, diet and glandular secretions. In the skin there are three kinds of glands that secrete directly onto the skin or into canals that lead to the skin surface, and some of these products are odorous. Skin products left on a glass slide by fingerprinting remain discernable to dogs for some weeks without specific preservation. The skin itself is a continuous source of 'rafts,' that is, dead

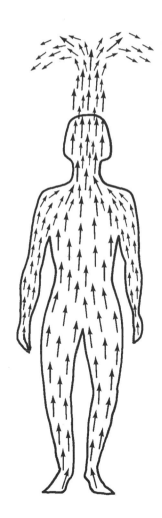

Air currents around the human body. According to Syrotuck, this current has a speed of 2.3 km/h and carried rafts up to 40 cm above the head, after which, they fall down.

cells that flake off from the outside and are replaced from within. These are left on the objects a person touches, and if sufficient material is left behind, modern DNA technology can be used to analyze mitochondrial DNA sequences and thus identify the owner. The rafts also flake off into the air and are carried away with air currents, and a whole theory of trailing is based on these rafts. The air currents around the human body transport these dead skin flakes. According to Syrotuck, this current has a speed of 2.3 km/h and carried rafts up to forty centimeters above the head, from whence they fall down.

Individual Human Odor

In human odors we distinguish odors from body openings, human skin, perspiration glands and sebaceous (sebum) glands. Furthermore, are other scents that can affect the human odor, just like soaps, medicines, etc.

- ### *Influencing Odors*
People with certain occupations, like butchers, bakers, farmers or working in labs or factories will have, in their clothes and shoes, specific occupational odors. The use of soap, foot powders and certain medicines will also have their influence on human odor.

- ### *Body Openings*
Odors from orifices such as, mouth, nose, ears, anus and uro-genital area also influence the individual human odor. Maybe not in the scent complex of a human track, but these odors can play a role with the work of search and rescue dogs – for example, while searching for people under rubble and snow. In particular, the breath and sometimes urine lost from panic or excitement can be an important odor source for the dog.

- ### *Human Skin*
The skin is an organ that protects against influences from outside. The upper, or outside layer, is called the Epidermis and consists of two types of cells: the Melanocytes, which are the pigment cells, and the Keratinocytes. In the basal

The top layers of human skin cells gradually flatten, shrink and lay more loosely against each other. They become keratin and this peels off at a rate of 0.5 to 1 g per day. Left: rafts that flake off; middle: releasing flakes; right: vapor and dead cells with bacteria on it.

layers of the skin, the Stratum Germinativum, Columnar Epithelial cells are found that divide and move outwards. These cells pass through several cell layers to the surface, called the Stratum Corneum. During this process, they first grow, then form Keratohyalin, and finally die. It is thought that the lipids in the Stratum Corneum form the physical skin barrier. These lipids are free fatty acids, cholesterol and ceramides. In the Stratum Corneum, the cells gradually flatten, shrink, and lay more loosely against each other. They become Keratin and this peels off at a rate of 0.5 to 1 g dead skin cells (rafts) per day. The Epidermis varies in thickness, but is normally only some tenths of a millimeter thick, no more than a thin membrane. On places where the skin has a lot of callus, like the palms of the hand and the soles of the feet, the epidermis is much thicker. As a result, of the continuous renewal of the epidermal cells from within and the peeling off on the outer surface renews about once a month. The rafts that flake off from the outer surface are normally invisible, except on the scalp as dandruff and as a consequence of certain skin diseases such as Psoriasis.

The second layer is called the Corium (or Dermis), and together with the Epidermis, these two layers form the skin. The corium is a one to three millimeter thick layer of connective tissue. Immediately below the Epidermis is the Papillary Dermis, and its contact area with the epidermis is a wavy pattern with bulges. Through these bulges the layers are connected with each other: they are filled with blood vessels (Capillaries) that provide food to the epidermis, and transport offal away. Further down in the Corium is the Reticular Dermis, which is the bulk of the Corium. These contain a network of bigger blood and lymph vessels, which also supply the Sebaceous and sweat glands, and the muscles around the hairs. The Reticular Dermis is characterized by dense collagen and elastic connective tissue. The blood vessels in the skin are not only responsible for providing nourishment and oxygen, but they also regulate the body temperature. In the Corium there are also a large number of nerve ends, which control the senses of touch, pain and temperature.

Underneath these layers is the Subcutis with the fatty tissue, which have important functions in heat insulation, energy storage and as a physical buffer.

• *Skin Glands*

In the skin we find, beside hair follicles and the places where nails are formed, sweat glands and sebum glands that secrete onto the skin, and therefore contribute to the odor on the skin. The sweat glands can be divided into Eccrine and Apocrine glands.

The two to four million Eccrine sweat glands occur all over the body and they produce a clear, watery solution. For the most part (more than 98 %) this solution consists of water, in which numerous organic and inorganic components are dissolved. The presence of these substances causes a reduction in sweat vapor pressure. The Eccrine sweat plays a major role in the thermoregulation of the body. Because of body warmth, and the air current around the body, the sweat solution evaporates immediately after it leaves the pores and comes out on the skin. During heavy sweating, it will be absorbed by the clothes that touch the skin. In emotional or nervous moments the Eccrine glands in the forehead, the palms of the hands, and the soles of the feet secrete a very large amount of sweat. In normal individuals, the glands can secrete as much as two to four liters per hour. The Apocrine glands are found in specific places on the human body, especially in the armpits and the genital area. They produce a cloudy, viscous solution containing large amounts of cholesterol. Bacteria on the skin break down Apocrine sweat into odorous molecules, in particular steroids, which are thought to be biologically interesting signals. According to Spielman and his collegues, the armpits, where the Apocrine glands are abundant, are even the source of human primer-type pheromones, the volatile smell substances that serve to get the attention of the other gender. He finds support for this in the similarity of the chemistry with non-human mammalian signaling odors. The auxiliary organ, as this bundling of Apocrine glands is called, is not equally present in all human races: Eastern races have small or even absent auxiliary organs, whereas on the other end of the scale certain Negroid groups have extremely large auxiliary organs. These glands in the armpits are the major source of body odor as perceived by other people. The difference in gland size is probably the reason why Negroids have a strong body odor to European noses, and Europeans in their turn smell noticeably different

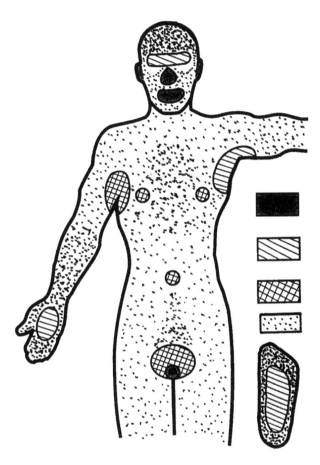

Distribution of the different sweat glands over the human body. Black: odors from bodily openings; striped: eccrine glands (influenced by emotions); crossed: apocrine sweat glands; pointed: eccrine sweat glands.

to Japanese noses.

The Sebaceous glands occur all over the body except on the palms of the hands and the soles of the feet. They always lie beside a hair follicle and discharge into that structure. The Sebum produces a seal for the hair shafts, preventing the penetration of bacteria, and also prevents a loss of fluid. Sebum consists of all sorts of fatty substances that keep the skin pliable and protect it against dehydrating. The products of the Sebaceous glands are spread all over the body by movement and that way they also arrive at the palms of the hands and the soles of the feet. On average there are about a hundred Sebaceous glands per square centimeter. On the middle of the chest and the back, also on the face and on the scalp, this amount will increase to almost a thousand. Humans with a high Sebum production often have problems with greasy hair. Sebum is discharged into a canal in the skin by a complete breakdown of the gland cell. In the canal, the Sebum and the remains of the cell are broken down by Lypolisis, by enzymes derived from the epidermis and bacteria. It takes eight to ten days from formation of the cell until the final breakdown of its products. The greatest part being Triglycerides and free fatty acids are found on the skin. These fatty acids are thought to form the olfactory signature of an individual. Support for this comes from examining scent-marking glands in other mammals: glands that are known to provide information about the identity of an individual. Rates of Sebum excretion, the ratio of wax esters to cholesterol, and cholesterol esters have been shown to change with age.

- ***Odor Production***

The skin's Microflora is essentially composed of such bacteria as Micrococcadeae, Staphylococci, Corynebacterium acnes, Pityrosporum Ovale, Pityrosporum acnes, Pityrosporum Granulosum, and Propionibacteria. Several studies have shown that treatment of the skin with antibiotics decreases the bacterial populations, and to a concurrent loss of fatty acids. However, some bacteria remain unaffected, probably because they are present in the hair follicles and out of reach for the skin antibiotics. Different populations are found in different body areas, but these populations remain quite stable in time. The consequence of these regional differences is that different body areas of the same person have different odors. The regions with the largest amounts of bacteria are the face, the neck, the armpits and the groin, but also on the soles of the feet and between the toes. The differences in bacterial population between people are quite large. With increasing age, the skin's Microflora undergoes qualitative changes. This is probably linked to hormonal changes and changes in Sebum production. The Streptococci found in children disappear and Coryneform bacteria increases. These are mainly responsible for odor production. Anaerobic Propionibacteria are more numerous in juveniles and young adults. And only Coryneform bacteria are able to produce the typical auxiliary odor by decomposition of Apocrine sweat. Coccids, however, don't have this capacity.

The prime candidate for olfactory individuality seems to be the lipids on human skin, which are, for the greater part, breakdown products of Sebum produced by Sebaceous glands. A small part comes from the epidermis and from contamination, but the production far outweighs the latter and a normal frequency of washing minimizes contamination. The Sebaceous glands are Holocrine glands, so some of the lipids in the Sebum are cell lipids (or epidermal lipids) and others are specialized lipids synthesized by the cell (Endogeneous lipids.) This synthesized part is thought to be the major influence on the composition of the secreted Sebum. Approximately 37 % of the fatty acids found on the skin are 'biologically valuable'; the remaining 63 % consists of more than two hundred different kinds of free fatty acids ranging from very small to very large (C7 – C30.) Some of these are very unusual, for example Sebaleic acid seems to be unique to the surface lipid of human skin (Schoon & Haak).

The chemical content of the skin lipids changes with age. In 2001, Robert Ramotowski summarized these changes that include rates of Sebum secretion and the amounts of certain fatty acids, but concludes that some components do not show significant change. Young children do not produce much Sebum, and the lipid composition is dominated by cholesterol and cholesterol esters, that are primarily of epidermal origin. As hormonal stimulation increases in puberty, more Sebum is produced up to peak production in mid-thirties. Women have lower secretion levels than males, and people with acne have higher secretions levels than people without acne. The stimulation of the Sebaceous glands results in a change in lipid composition on the skin: more endogenously produced lipids are found, the epidermal lipids remain relatively constant. Overall, the secretion levels and Sebum composition remain constant from puberty until much later in life (males over seventy, females over fifty.) The principle reason behind this decline is diminished hormonal stimulation.

By comparing lipid composition between identical twins and unrelated people, evidence for genetic control of the lipid composition was found. A large body of work on genetic control of urine odors has shown the significant role of the major histocompatability complex (MHC). This MHC is a group of genes connected to the immune system. In humans it is called HLA and the genes are located on Chromosome 7. Recent theories are based on interactions between immune system antigens and bacteria. The antigens (or their break-down products) could influence the commensal bacterial flora and thus the individual body odor. This study area could be important for forensic scientist working with odors, as Dr. Boyse said: 'odor profiles governed by HLA could be more distinctive than fingerprints with respect to genetic identity, because the genetic component of fingerprints is uncertain.'

As a result of regional differences in microflora on the skin, different body parts have their own particular odor. To humans, the odor in the armpit smells totally different than that in the genital area, and this in turn smells different from the soles of the feet. In fact, Dr. Löhner found that for humans the similarity between the same regions of different people seems to be greater than different regions of the same person. This does not mean that a common factor does not exist; in fact, Löhner himself found that for dogs the similarity in different body areas of the same person was greater than similarity in odor between the same areas belonging to different people. There is also some evidence that this capacity to focus on the common odor is the result of training: Dr. Brisbin and Dr. Austad found that dogs trained to detect the hand-odor of their handler had difficulty in choosing between the hand-odor of a stranger and odors from different regions of their handler. Matching objects scented in pockets to the hand-odor of the same individual is much more accurate than those where the hand odor had to be matched to another part of the body, such as the crook of the elbow.

The importance of genetics in human odor is also evident from behavioral studies where the difference between the odors of identical twins, siblings or other genetically related people is smaller than differences between odors of non-related people. The stability of this typical odor is also clear from these studies: siblings recognize each other's odor on a T-shirt after not having seen each other for more than two years. It is now generally accepted that there is a genetic base for unique human odor.

• *Stability of Odor*
For forensic purposes, the stability of the odor is an important factor. Although

On overgrown, moistened soil, a well-trained dog can work out a track up to 36 hours old.

no experiments have been undertaken to try to specifically alter an individual's odor, it seems unlikely that such changes can occur easily: if a person's genetic makeup influences the microflora responsible for the composition of fatty acids on his skin, the only way would be to purposely change one's bacterial microflora. Minimizing auxiliary odor by modifying the microflora would produce less odor, however, the continuing source of income for the pharmaceutical and cosmetics industries illustrates the difficulty of such actions. Application of antibiotics onto the skin does influence the bacterial population and can diminish their amounts. However, these are usually only applied locally, and the larger part of the body continues to function as before. Although diet seems to have an effect on the odor of an individual, dietary lipids are the minority in the skin lipids and the long turnover time of the Sebaceous cells (approximately eight to ten days) prevents major effects. Trace amounts of nicotine, morphine, alcohol and steroids have been observed. Washing would minimize the amount of lipids on the skin, but the effect is short-term since the lipids are replenished quickly. Behavioral studies confirm the stability of odors in humans.

The odor traces left on objects connected to a crime must also be stable, since the period of time between depositing the odor by the perpetrator and the comparison with the odor of a suspect can be considerable. The stability of scents produced by Sebaceous glands can be deduced from the fact that scent marks that need to stay around for a long time are produced by Sebaceous glands, but even so there is a 'temporal aspect' to odor signals. Direct sunlight, in particular, breaks down many organic substances, and some micro-organisms. In a study done by the Pacific Northwest National Laboratory, described by Robert Ramatowski, the chemical changes in latent fingerprint deposits show that saturated fatty compounds remain relatively stable. However, unsaturated lipids, such as Squalene and some of the fatty acids, diminished substantially within a thirty day period, especially during the first week. With time, more saturated low-molecular acids appeared, originating from the breaking down of the unsaturated lipids. In aged samples, the saturated components dominate.

The essential question for forensic purposes is how long human odor would retain its unique identity for a dog. The fingerprint study is confirmed of scent identifications made by dog instructors in teaching a dog to make matches based on aged. Objects aged up to a week require the dog to be trained stepwise and seem to be relatively difficult. Once objects are older than a week, they are no longer a problem. Dogs can manage much older objects with the same ease.

Dog's Scent Perception

All living creatures give off odorants by their metabolism, respiration, glandular secretions, etc., by which every living being acquires his own individual odor. These odorants can periodically be of a different strength and composition. Dogs can observe organic connections in human sweat diluted a million-fold.

On moistened sand, well-trained dogs can work out a track about twelve hours old and on overgrown, moistened soil up to thirty six hours. Even if the track is washed out by heavy rainfall and after intensive radiation from the sun, scent perception is still strong up to six hours later.

The sense of smell, just like the sense of taste, is a chemical sense. This is because prickles are characterized by chemicals, with which these substances, in liquid or gas form, exert their influence on the sense. A sense is an organ that can detect prickles from the outside world (for instance, recognizing prey or an enemy) or prickles from the body itself (hunger). These prickles then are changed into a signal the brain can understand which then provides the right response for the animal.

• *Inside the Dog's Nose*

Inside the dog's nose are two kinds of Epithelium: the Respiratory Epithelium and the Olfactory Epithelium. The Respiratory Epithelium has small hairs and is coated with mucus. Its function is to clean incoming air, to moisten it and to warm the air breathed in to body temperature. The Olfactory Epithelium is located deep inside the nose, next to the Cribiform Plate and is darkly pigmented. It covers the large surface of a number of bony plates called Ethmoid bones.

The Olfactory Epithelium differs in size across different kinds of animals. There is also a variation in sizes between the Olfactory Epithelium of different breeds of dogs, but there is no direct link between the size of the dog and the size of its Olfactory Epithelium. Besides this, there is no simple relationship between the size of the Olfactory Epithelium and sensitivity to odors. An animal with a large Olfactory Epithelium is not automatically more sensitive to odors than an animal with a smaller one. A German Shepherd has an Olfactory Epithelium that is 150 – 170 cm2, humans have an Olfactory Epithelium of approximately 5 cm2. Some odors can be smelled equally well by man and dog, but for other odors dogs are 10 000 times more sensitive than humans.

An important and unique characteristic of the Olfactory Epithelium is its continuous regeneration: neurons in the epithelium live thirty to sixty days at which point they die, and then are replaced with new neurons. This means that when the Olfactory Epithelium is damaged, it can completely recover in one to two months. This ability to regenerate is not present in the same way as in other sensory organs.

Odor molecules can reach the Olfactory Epithelium by way of the nose or the mouth. The Olfactory Epithelium is covered with mucus. In this mucus there are small hairs (Cilia), and on these hairs are the olfactory receptors. The Cilia are extensions from the olfactory sensory neurons in the epithelium. The density of these sensory neurons differs between species, and also changes during the lifetime of an animal. When a young animal grows up, the density of the sensory neurons (and the sensitivity to odors) first increases; when an animal becomes

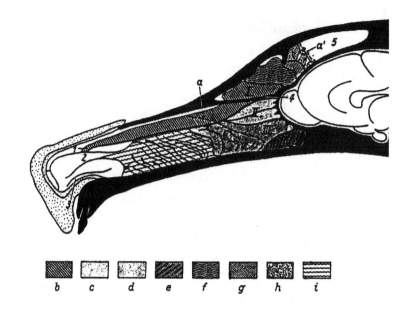

Cross section of the olfactory organ of a dog.
(From: Nickel, Schummer and Seiferle).
a-a': boundaries of the olfactory epithelium;
I-IV and b-e: endoterminal plates; f-h:
ectoterminal plates; b, c and i: nasal cavity;
1-5: bones.

really old, the density (and the sensitivity) decreases. Besides the olfactory sensory neurons, the Olfactory Epithelium also contains supporting cells and basal cells. The sensory neurons terminate in a nerve that passes through the Cribiform plate to the olfactory bulb in the brain. In the brain the nerves are bundled in nerve knots called Glomeruli.

Deep inside the nose, many animals, including dogs, have a second organ that is sensitive to odors, called the Vomeronasal Organ. The Vomeronasal Organ is situated above the roof of the mouth and in the nose-mouth cavity. The organ is very small and difficult to localize, which is why it was ignored for a long time. The sensory cells in the epithelium of the Vomeronasal Organ have different receptors than those in the Olfactory Epithelium of the nose. In the Vomeronasal Organ, there are approximately one hundred different kinds of receptors. Odors do not reach the Vomeronasal Organ by chance. A number of animals show typical behaviors, such as after an animal has licked the source of an odor; they curl their upper lip in such a way that the nostrils are blocked, also known as 'flehmen' – a typical smelling behavior that has also been described for other animals. It appears that physical contact with the odor source is necessary for transport into the Vomeronasal Organ. The probable function of the Vomeronasal Organ is a sexual one: detecting so-called 'pheromones.' Pheromones are odors that have a strong biological

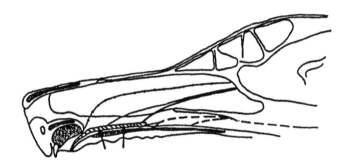

The vomeronasal organ in the nasal cavity, located by arrows (From: Salazar, Barber and Cifuentes).

significance for an animal. They contain information about sex, and reproductive state. These odors can also lead to physiological changes in an animal. Examples can be found in animals and people. In humans, females that have regular odor contact with males have a shorter menstrual cycle than females who do not. The menstrual cycles of women who live together, for example nuns, or students who live in all-female housing on campus, become synchronized, and it seems this is regulated by odor cues.

• *Odor Contacts Receptor*

In the air, odor molecules float around and the odor receptors that react to these molecules are hidden deep inside the nose. The main route for these molecules is through the nose, but odor molecules can also travel from the mouth, such instances as, during eating – they can travel up through the throat to the nasal cavity to the odor receptors. When sitting calmly, a dog breathes in and out approximately fifteen times per minute. When walking calmly, the frequency rises to thirty one times per minute. During this ordinary action of respiratory breathing, the largest amount of air goes to the lungs via the quickest route, and the odor molecules in this air do not actively pass by the odor receptors in the Olfactory Epithelium. With normal breathing, odor molecules will only reach this area if the concentration in the air is very high. For both humans and dogs it is known that odor molecules reach the Olfactory Epithelium by active sniffing. When a dog sniffs, the inhalation/exhalation

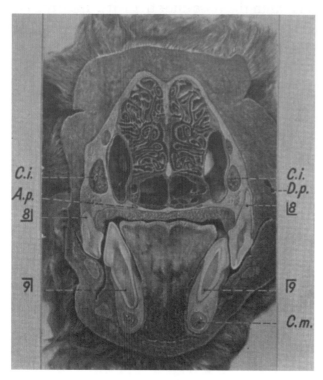

Transverse section of the muzzle near the canines in the upper and lower jaw of a ten-month-old Airedale Terrier female. In the upper part the right and left nasal cavities and the with mucous membrane covered conchae maxillaris are visible. (From: J. Bodingbauer).

frequency rises to one hundred and forty to two hundred times per minute. The sniffing leads to differences in air pressure in the nose. The total result is that the air, with the odor molecules in it, enters deep into all the nasal cavities.

In tracking dogs and trailing dogs, another breathing technique that leads to scent perception can be described. This is called 'air scenting': one long inhalation, lasting twenty times longer than the ordinary breathing frequency. During this long nasal inhalation, the dogs exhale through their mouth. This method probably leads to an optimal presentation of odor molecules to the receptors in the Olfactory Epithelium. Measurements on breathing pattern of dogs during tracking have revealed that with increasing difficulty of the track, the dogs increase their sniffing frequency. The duration of the sniffing bouts increased.

The odor receptors are located on Cilia in the mucus that covers the Olfactory Epithelium. This mucus is watery and contains different agents that cleanse the air, for example it contains antibodies to different bacteria, and detoxifying enzymes. To reach the olfactory receptors, the odor molecules must first dissolve in this watery mucus. However, a characteristic of odor molecules is that they do not dissolve well in water. The mucus contains certain proteins, called 'olfactory binding proteins' that function as carriers. The odor molecules are attached to these proteins, then dissolve in the

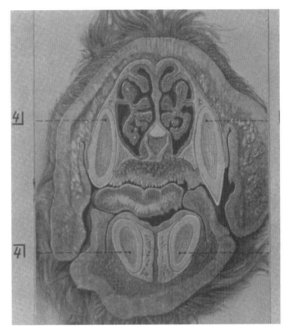

Transverse section of the muzzle of the same Airedale Terrier female, but here near the first molar in the upper jar, and the fourth premolar teeth in the lower jar. Remarkable is the extension of the with olfactory epithelium covered conchae ethmoidalis.
(From: J. Bodingbauer).

mucus, and are transported to the olfactory receptors.

There are probably around 1 000 different kinds of receptors. Research done with dogs has shown that there are no differences between breeds on this point. For comparison: the eye has three different kinds of receptors that make it possible for us to see the variety of color that we do. The tongue has four kinds of receptors that give us our taste sensations.

Every olfactory sensory neuron has several Cilia with receptors. The Cilia of a single olfactory sensory neuron are believed to have the same one kind of olfactory receptor. The olfactory sensory neurons that carry the Cilia, and therefore also the receptors, live for thirty to sixty days. After this they die, and new neurons are made. At some stage during the development of a new neuron, the type of receptor for this neuron is determined. If a neuron with receptor type A has died, this does not automatically lead to a new neuron with receptor type A. The determination of the receptor type is partly triggered by the odors the animal often smells. Animals that have been systematically trained on certain odors develop more receptors for these odors.

Each olfactory sensory neuron reacts to different odors. Every odor stimulates different kinds of odor receptors. It is probable that each type of receptor reacts to a certain part of an odor molecule: a certain shape, or chemical group. Each odor stimulates a different group. In this way 1 000 different kinds of odor receptors can differentiate clearly between a large amount of odors. The odor receptors are not spread evenly over the Olfactory Epithelium, but are divided into at least four zones. This is also known of other receptors: the taste receptors for 'bitter' are located in a band across the hind part of the tongue, the receptors for 'sweet' on the tip of the tongue, and for 'acid' on the sides.

• *From Nose to Brain*

When the receptor reacts to an odor signal, the olfactory sensory neuron 'fires' an impulse that is carried through the nerve to the Bulbus Olfactorius in the brain. The Bulbus Olfactorius is the olfactory centre of the brain. It is located directly behind the Cribiform Plate. The connection between the brain and the receptor is extremely short: the same sensory neuron that has the receptors on Cilia at one end, is the neuron, or nerve, that delivers the impulse to the brain. This is unique to the olfactory system: in all other sensory organs the signal is first passed on to another nerve, and sometimes this takes place several times, before the signal reaches the brain.

The olfactory nerves converge to 1 000 – 2 000 nerve-knots called Glomeruli in the first layer of the Bulbus Olfactorius. The nerve ends of sensory cells that have the same kind of olfactory receptor all come together in the same Glomerulus. Sensory cells of a certain receptor type therefore have a matching Glomerulus in the brain. Because the information from many olfactory sensory neurons comes together in a single matching Glomerulus in

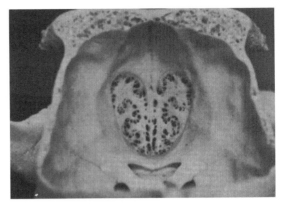

A dog's cribiform plate of the ethmoid bone from inside the skull. Through openings the olfactory nerves from below enters the brain. According to the enormous amount of olfactory nerves, the cribiform plate of the dog is very large. (From: J. Bodingbauer).

the brain, the signal is amplified. Even if only a few sensory cells are triggered by an odor, the information is bundled in the first layer of Glomeruli in the olfactory brain and this layer can then project a clear signal to the second layer of Glomeruli deeper in the Bulbus Olfactorius.

In the Olfactory Epithelium, sensory cells of the same receptor-type are distributed evenly within a zone. Each zone in the epithelium connects with a zone in the Bulbus Olfactorius. Sensory cells of the same receptor type all connect to the same Glomeruli. In this manner a clear spatial pattern emerges: each odor stimulates a characteristic of a spatial pattern of Glomeruli in the brain.

The development of the Glomeruli in the Bulbus Olfactorius is partly determined by which odors an animal comes across. By training a young animal on an odor, it develops more olfactory sensory neurons for that particular odor and the matching Glomerules also becomes more developed.

The information from the first layer of Glomeruli in the Bulbus Olfactorius is passed on to a second layer of Glomeruli. The Glomeruli in this second layer is interconnected, which leads to a better perception of minute differences. This makes the signal clearer. The Glomeruli in this second layer are also influenced by experience.

- *Limbic System vs. Cortex*

The signals from the Bulbus Olfactorius follow two paths for further processing in the brain. One path leads to the Cortex, which is the most outward part of the brain. In this area of the brain the animal first becomes 'aware' of the odor, he then perceives the odor, finally recognizing the odor, and reacts or doesn't react, according to his understanding of this odor. This process is called the cognitive processing of the information.

The other path leads deep into the brain to an area called the Limbic System. The Limbic System is responsible for many autonomic processes – processes we are not conscious of. It influences different physiological processes, emotions and sexual behavior. The Limbic System receives odor-information through the main olfactory epithelium, but also from the Vomeronasal Organ. Experiments with humans have shown that even though a brain reacts to an odor, this does not mean that this person is conscious of smelling something. The processing of olfactory information by the Limbic System is called the non-cognitive processing.

Odors can have great physical impact on the animal through the Limbic System. The odor of lemons counters depression in rats. The odor of a human male shortens the menstrual cycle of the human female. The odor of a strange male leads to a spontaneous abortion in a rat that has just become pregnant by another male. Some odors stimulate animals, others slow them down.

The processing of information by the Limbic System is fast: it takes place before the processing in the cortex. This means that the non-cognitive effects of odors through the Limbic System may interfere with the cognitive processing in the cortex. A good example from police practice is the reaction of a dog to the odor of the kennel staff. Using the odor of kennel staff as foils in a scent identification line-up often leads to mistakes. This can be explained by the direct

Chapter 6

Using members of the kennel staff for cross-tracks often leads to mistakes. This can be explained by the direct positive association the dog has with this person's odor: food, being taken for a walk, attention, etc. The dog can react to this odor before he 'realizes' he is actually looking for a different odor. And the mistake is made.

positive association the dog has with these people's odor: food, being taken for a walk, and general attention they give to the dogs. The dog can react to this odor before he 'realizes' he is actually looking for a different odor. And the mistake is made. The reverse problem can also be explained in this way: maybe an odor that the dog finds very 'difficult' is an odor he has a very negative association with, leading to avoidance behavior.

Another example is the reaction of a male dog to the scent of a bitch in heat. This odor initiates the whole sexual behavior pattern through the Limbic

System. Even though a dog can be taught not to do this, the first reaction to the odor will always be there: the procreation drive of all normal animals.

As is clear from everything written before, the olfactory organ is not static but changes. It is continuously regenerated and it reacts to differences in the environment. When an animal is confronted with a certain odor, this often leads to physical differences in the olfactory organ. These changes can be seen on all levels: more sensory cells with the right kind of receptor, larger Glomeruli, permanent changes in the brain. Reversely, when an animal never comes into contact with odors, this leads to a poor development of the olfactory organ.

Chapter 7:
Scent Problems and Training Problems

In general, all sensory organs work in the same way: Each sense organ has receptors. These receptors are located in or on sensory neurons. The receptors react to a signal in the environment. This signal stimulates the sensory neuron, and results in an impulse in the sensory neuron. This impuls can be seen as an electric current, running from the sensory neuron through the nerves. The impulse can be transmitted from one nerve to the other, until it reaches the brain and the information is processed.

Problems in the Olfactory Organ

PROBLEMS IN PERCEPTION CAN OCCUR at any stage. Here are some of the major problems that you are most likely to encounter when the Olfactory organ of a dog is not responding:

- the signal cannot reach the receptor;
- there is no receptor available for a certain kind of signal;
- the sensory neuron does not react;
- the nerve does not react;
- the brain interprets the information incorrectly.

The number of olfactory receptors for a particular scent is adjusted to how often this scent is smelled. This implies that to optimize the nose of your dog, you need continuous scent-training.

Every olfactory sensory neuron has a single kind of olfactory receptor. Olfactory receptors are continuously renewed together with their olfactory sensory neuron. The number of olfactory receptors for a particular scent is adjusted to how often this scent is smelled. An animal has a lot of olfactory receptors for scents that he smells regularly. This implies that to optimize the nose of your dog, you need continuous scent-training.

Odor and Odorless

It is relatively easy to prove that something has an odor: if a person can smell it, or if you can train an animal to react to it based on odor, then it has an odor. But it is much more difficult to prove that something has no odor at all. Maybe a person with a very sensitive nose could smell it, or maybe the animal you trained was not trained correctly.

And there is another problem. In research with people, characteristic brain

Chapter 7

Many dog handlers have made the mistake of punishing their dogs because they thought that there was no more odor present, to discover later that in all probability there was an odor left on that place.

wave patterns were established using EEG when people smelled an odor. It then appeared that sometimes a person's brain reacts in this characteristic way to an odor, but the person himself will say he has not smelled anything.

So, we must be aware that terms like 'odor' and 'odorless' are difficult to define and we must use them with care. A lot of substances that are odorless for people can be perceived by dogs. Odorless doesn't really exist. Everything has at least its own scent!

To clean an object of an odor it is not enough to boil it in water, since odor molecules do not dissolve well in water. It is necessary to use (non-perfumed) soap or other fat-dissolving products.

Furthermore, there are certain porous substances which can absorb and retain odor (sometimes for a long time). Many dog handlers have made the mistake of punishing their dogs because they thought that there was no more odor present, to discover later that in all probability there was an odor left on that place. You can't be positive that your problem with odor is because there isn't one there. Keep in mind the possibility of 'disturbing', 'related' or 'remnant' odors.

Temperature and Scent

Temperature plays an important role in the perception of scents. Warm substances (or articles) give off more scent in cold surroundings than warm substances in hot surroundings. Cold articles are more difficult to find in cold surroundings.

Substances or articles that already give off recognizable scent under normal circumstances smell stronger when they become warmer. Warm food smells, as you know, much stronger than a cold meal.

Extreme cold can cut back the concentration of smellable gasses to hardly perceptible amounts (like the difference between a hot steak or one which is frozen). But all frozen things give off some recognizable scent, so minute amounts of gas are released, which are warmed up in the nose and penetrate the receptors in the olfactory epithelium.

Alternating Perception

In humans, every few hours the nostrils alternate. They are closed in turn by a light swelling and the closed nostril lets pass less air than the other nostril. According to Noam Sobel and his colleagues of the Berkeley University of California these changes in air current also have consequences for scent discrimination. He gave twenty test persons a mix of carvon (found in caraway and the rind of mandarin) and octane (which smells like petroleum) to smell. Seventeen of the twenty persons found the mix smelled more like carvon than octane, when they smelled with the 'active' nostril, and the opposite when they used the inactive one. After a few hours, as the nostrils alternated, the same happened, which proofs that the differences in smell were not caused by just the left or right nostril. These alternations also can happen in the dog's nose, although it has not been researched until now.

Smelling Problems

There are some problems in perceiving scents caused by the physical condition of the dog:
- Common cold or influenza.
- Certain illnesses.
- Medication.
- Genetic effects.
- Dental problems.
- Hormonal circumstances.
- Albino and light colored dogs.
- Short nosed breeds.
- Small breeds.

In some cases it will be difficult or even impossible for the dog to perceive scents. Common colds, or even the influenza virus, can affect the sense of smell. Humans with these illnesses, as well as dogs, can have a decreased ability to perceive scents. It is known that dogs that have been infected by the influenza virus, but who do not yet show the normal symptoms, already have a lower olfactory sensitivity. Even the beginning of an infection such as kennel cough can lead to a diminished sense of smell. There are also other ilnesses that can diminish the olfactory system of the dog, for example, renal failure, Cushing's syndrome (an adrenal hypersecretion), hypothyriodism, etc. Of course, certain medications (f.i. antibiotics) can affect the ability to smell.

In people we know that some humans cannot perceive certain scents, and therefore significant genetic effects were found. Problems in the upper teeth, like root infections, scale on teeth or a poor breath, can influence the ability of the dog to smell.

In general, female dogs have a more acute sense of smell than males, although hormonal circumstances can influence their scent perception.

The short nosed breeds often experience problems with search work because of respiration problems. Boxers, for instance, can track as well as other working dogs, but on long tracks they need more stops to rest.

Oncoming heat, or being on heat itself, can affect both the sense of smell and the concentration of the bitch. A bitch on heat in the neighborhood, or changes in the pack order can also affect the dogs.

The ability to smell of albino and certain white or light colored dogs can be diminished in part, or in full. That may also be why albino animals in the wild hardly have a chance to survive; partly because of their marked white color and on the other hand because they are unable to distinguish scents well enough.

The short nosed breeds often experience problems with search work because of respiration problems. Boxers, for instance, can track as well as other working dogs, but on long tracks they need more stops to rest. The smaller breeds are thought to have a theoretical disadvantage, because they have a smaller olfactory area. In practice, however, it has been shown that the little breeds can easily perform as good search dogs.

Adaptation and Nose-fatigue

The precise way in which a scent signal triggers a reaction in the olfactory receptor is unknown. In some way this scent signal leads to the 'firing' of an 'impulse', which can be compared to an electric current that is transmitted through the long nerve all the way to the brain. When a certain sensory cell is continuously being triggered to fire, it begins to adapt to this situation. Adaptation is the 'adjustment of the sensory cell to weaker or stronger sensory signals'. If a sensory cell is continuously stimulated in a certain way, it will cease to react to this stimulus. An example: if you enter a room where people are smoking, you notice this when you come in, but after a while you don't notice it any more. If you go out, and let your nose 'rest' for a bit, you can smell the smoke again. Such an adaptation is also a fact with dogs!

The slow adaptation is a mental 'tiredness', also called 'nose-fatigue'.

To be clear: We, and also our dogs, are not smelling with our nose, because the olfactory epithelium is only an organ to scan. The prickles coming in via the cilia turn into signals, which the smell fibres (fila olfactoria) will bring to the olfactory bulb. The brains take care that these signals lead to the right scent

When a dog is tracking with his nose deep down exactly on the track, his nose can also adapt to this odor. By deviating from the track the dog may 'clear his nose' and be able to smell the scent on the track again.

impression. We are in fact smelling with our brains!

The adaptation in the olfactory system is manifested at two levels. The fast adaptation (in less then one second) is the quick change from phasic to tonic response during continuous stimulation, which is physical and happens at the sensory neuron level. Fast adaptation may be related to the decrease (within a fraction of a second) of scent perception upon cessation of breathing during a sniff, documented by R.W. Moncrieff.

When the scent is removed from the air over the epithelium after long stimulation, the sensory response diminishes from tonic level to zero within a few hundred milliseconds. Such relatively fast turnoff is essential for a sensory mechanism that responds to changes occuring between consecutive sniffs.

The second level is the slow adaptation (in about one minute), which is a mental 'tiredness', also called 'nose-fatigue'. This is the slow suppression of perceived odor intensity during prolonged exposure arising from central neuronal processing.

When working with police dogs, you can come across situations where adaptation plays a role. Here are some examples:

- The density of narcotic scent for example in a room where a lot of a certain narcotic has been hidden, or where a smaller amount has been hidden for a long time, can be very high. In such a situation a dog may have problems in indicating the exact source of the scent, especially if he has been in the room for some time. This can be explained by adaptation: the sensory cells of the dog have been stimulated so much that they no longer react to this smell. Of course, lack of a gradient in such an odor-saturated environment can also explain why the dog can not locate the source. Dogs know by themselves how to handle this situation: they want to go outside to get a breath of fresh air, and then come inside again. In some cases this has to happen moretimes before the dog can pin-point the correct spot of the scent.
- When a search and rescue dog locates an odor in the rubble, it sometimes can happen that the dog goes away from that place, even shortly from the rubble, comes back to that place again with a better perception and can better pin-point the scent clue.
- When a dog is tracking with his nose deep down exactly on the track, his nose can also adapt to this odor. By deviating from the track the dog may 'clear his nose' and be able to smell the scent on the track again.

If you punish such acts, as sometimes happens in dogsport trainings, that will lead to the dog delivering less. Or he will put his nose to the ground and act as though he is searching or tracking, without doing so!

Chemical Blockers

Another aspect of adaptation is 'cross-adaptation'. This means that when adapted to a certain scent, it also becomes impossible to smell certain other scents. This phenomenon has been described a number of times for several scents, but not all cross-adaptations are known. Certain chemicals can block the largest part of the olfactory cells or push aside other scent substances. Examples of this are acetone and xylol. If you first smell acetone and then xylol, both scents can be very clearly perceived. The other way around, smelling the xylol first, the acetone cannot be perceived anymore for some time after.

Handlers of tracking dogs and detector dogs, like drug and explosive detector dogs, have to be aware of this phenomenon. They have to think about the fact that other substances, like ether or petrol, can fill up the nose with scent, so that the dog's nose can be more or less blocked for several minutes. To determine slighter scents becomes very difficult in that period.

The dog's ability to smell, the same as that of humans, will be disturbed by irritants, and strong and abnormal scent prickles. An example of this is tracking on a meadow strewn with fertilizer. Because of that, a professional handler must train his dog in all kind of situations and under constantly changing circumstances.

Scent and Memory

The sense of smell has also to do with learning and memory. Homesickness will occur in children partly because of unfamiliar odors. A way to prevent homesickness is to allow the child to take along a cuddle toy with an odor of home. Because of that, when you pick up a new puppy, you should request a toy or piece of cloth with the odor of the litter; it will put him at ease when he smells the well known odor among all the strange, new odors.

Where memory is concerned, everybody knows that odors not only bring back memories (which is true for every sense), but that smell prickles are very penetrative. There are cases of people who couldn't remember anything of nursery school untill they sniffed up a typical 'school odor'. Such an odor reminds us of earlier times and our memory can recall these images. Probably this recognition of odor also shows why a dog recognizes, often after many years, his previous owner.

Taste and smell have to develop, and some people are able to distinguish, while other people cannot, small differences in scent and taste, like, for instance, winemakers. When food storage was a big problem in the past, animals were used to pre-taste meals. Even now one can still see that a cat will not drink sour milk or eat bad meat.

It seems that astronauts feel awkward during their long travels because of the absence of odor. They tried to improve this by providing them with little bottles with nice, familiar odors, which they associated with good memories, that they could smell now and then.

Failure Scents

Dogs can connect certain problems in searching or tracking with a 'failure scent,' for instance with difficulties on a track and the smell of certain types of soil, or with the odor of certain tracklayers.

Another example of the relationship between smell and memory is the following: During tests, people were given a difficult task, which they couldn't do well, and at the same time they were exposed to an unusual scent. Subsequently, when they were asked to complete an easy, ordinary task, with the same scent present, they had difficulty succeeding with it. With conditioning, this scent had become associated with failure.

Dogs can make the same connections with certain problems during searching or tracking with such a failure scent, for instance with difficulties on a track and the smell of certain types of soil. Or with the odor of certain tracklayers!

Females' Sensitive Sense

The capability of an individual to smell varies in time and is influenced amongst others by hormonal variation, age and illness. In general, females of a species have a more sensitive sense of smell than males. Overall sensitivity decreases with age. But there are large individual differences: not only in people, but also in other animals such as dogs. A single individual may also differ in time, and react more sensitively at one time than at another. This can be the result of (amongst others) hormonal variation.

Amount of Scent

Another result of training animals on scents was that differences in amount of scent appeared to be perceived by the animals as differences in kind of scent: a lot of one scent simply smelled differently than a small amount of the same scent. This phenomenon is also known from hearing and seeing: a very loud C-tone sounds different from a very soft C-tone. Recently it was established that differences in amount of scent lead to qualitatively different processes in the brain. Therefore, a small amount of a scent does not lead to a less strong reaction than a large amount, but to a completely different reaction. This means that when training a dog on a scent, the amounts of scent used in the training must vary a lot: the dog may 'think' that a large amount of a scent is a completely different thing than a smaller amount of the same scent. When a dog is used only to find small amounts, he may not 'recognize' a large amount of the same. It simply smells different from what he has learned.

Chapter 7

When a dog is used only to find small amounts, he may
not 'recognize' a large amount of the same odor. It
simply smells something different from what he has
learned.

Complex Scents

In training animals to discriminate between scents it appeared that this was more difficult when the scents were complex (combinations of different scents) than when the scents were single scents. It was also shown that if a scent is presented alone, an animal is much more sensitive to the scent than if the same scent is presented as part of a complex. This is something to be aware of in training: if a dog is capable of finding a very small amount of a 'pure' material, he may still have problems when he has to find this same small amount as part of a complex material.

Finally it also appeared that complex scents are learned as a unit. If an animal has previous experience with single components in the complex, this did speed up the learning of these complex scents. Beginning the training of a dog with single scents must therefore lead to a more rapid learning of the complex compounds containing these single scents. But we cannot say that a dog, trained on the single scents, will always recognize these scents in complex compounds. A dog must also be trained on the complex compounds.

Extremely Strenuous

Intensive tracking requires concentrated muscular movements, in particular, because of the peculiar tensed way of walking of a dog.

Even under normal weather conditions search work is for the dog extremely strenuous, and the limits of a dog's physical stress are quickly reached. All kinds of scent detection work demand high neurological and cerebral activity from the dog, and for instance tracking is not a normal posture for him. Intensive tracking requires concentrated muscular movements, in particular because of the peculiar, tensed way of walking a stretched and bent posture forces onto a dog. That causes an extra load on the joints and the muscle activity produces pyruvate and lactate (lactic acid) in the muscular tissue (acidification). High demand are also made on respiration, heartbeat and body temperature. Research of Dr. Briewasser shows the effort the dog brings to search work. He tested experienced tracking dogs before and after working out a track of about 1000 paces long. Not only the body temperature rised considerable from

38.3° to 40.1° C (feaver!), but also the pulse rate rised from 92 to 142 , and respiration from 41 to 145 reached an absolute top-level.

So, intensive search work requires top mental and physical effort of the dog. Because of that, before start searching, if possible, do warm-up exercises, by which the animal can prepare itself mentally and physically. In his research Dr. Briewasser also determined that the temperature, respiration and pulse values from before the tracking were reached again some 1½ hour after tracking was over. This compares to studies in which the body temperature of a dog after a tracking exercise was increased to 41.86° C and ten minutes later was still 40.56° C. For that reason it is strongly recommend to walk with the dog in a relaxed way for five to ten minutes after search work and then give him at least 1½ hour rest, before starting other exercises.

Serious Problems

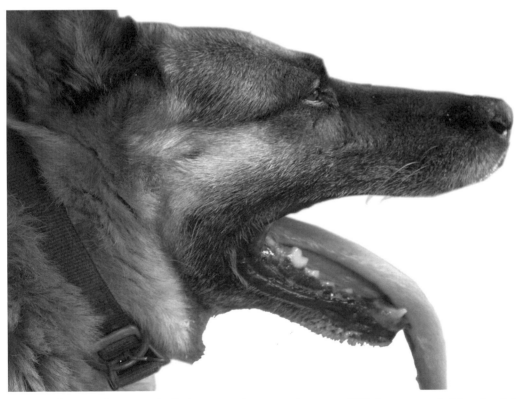

At environmental temperatures of over 28 C, especially in high humidity, the body temperature of the dog increases, which will be prevented by panting as much as possible.

Therapy consists of, first, doing things to decrease the body temperature.

At environmental temperatures over 28° C (especially in high humidity), the body temperature of the dog increases a bit, which will be prevented by panting as much as possible. If the environmental temperature increases, the body temperature of the dog also increases, in spite of his attempts to lose the superfluous heat in another way (for instance, by laying down on cold paving). Therapy consists of, first, doing things to decrease the body temperature: bringing the dog into the shade, or into a cool room (cellars), moistening the limbs with cold water, icepacks around the head and neck, carefully sprinkling the body with cold water, etc. If you do not discover in time that the dog's heat control is threatening to break down to collapse, the dog will quickly develop the clinical symptoms of heat stroke. The vicious circle is closed: The animal cannot shed all superfluous heat and his body temperature rises over 40° C. Because of dilating of peripheral capillaries, the total blood vessel volume is excessively increased, so the circulation fails. The pulse is irregular and weak, and often vomiting and diarrhoea occur. The dog is exhausted and becomes unconscious.

At a body temperature of 41.5° C, the dog is in serious trouble. The cerebral and spinal cord functions become disordered, the dog shows disturbance in movement, the heartbeat increases, and the dog breathes fast and deep. Unlike panting this fast, deep breathing is very hard on him.

Body temperatures of 42-43° C, even for a short time, are fatal for the dog. Animals that survive temperatures of 41° C can suffer permanent cerebral damage and cardiac arrythmia. Such dogs tire progressively more quickly and weaken in the limbs (particularly the hindquarters). They look they will faint and often we see the eyes of the dog rolling up. Every time it happens, the dog's body gets walloped. Finally the dog has to be withdrawn from operational service.

Motivation

All search work requires a dog to work independently and full of concentration. One cannot force a dog to do this: coercion only leads to a dog paying attention to the handler instead of to the scent involved. The dog has to enjoy the game, otherwise it is better to stop. Some dogs prefer other activities (tracking, scent line-ups, detection or protection work) and then a choice needs to be made. Performing search work has to be the nicest activity of the dog with his handler. Motivation can be influenced by the relation dog-handler, but also by physical problems (back pain, sore foot, ear infection, on heat or a bitch on heat in the neighborhood). Establish the cause of a lack of motivation, have patience, an adjust your training.

It is advantageous to work in a group and to discuss problems prior to doing something about them. Others often see things a handler himself has not yet noticed. Discussing and thoroughly analyzing a problem often leads to a direct solution.

Systematic Mistakes

There are also systematic oddities a dog can learn to react to. For example, if the matching odor in a scent identification line-up is always collected last in the series, or when this person is asked to give odor for a longer period of time. This leads to the scent picture of the matching odor to be fresher, or stronger, than the other odors in the line-up. If this is done in a systematic way, the dog can learn to react to this difference, since following this 'fresh, strong odor' strategy leads to a reward. Dutch police dog handlers are very aware of this danger and take sufficient precautions, which are also part of the official regulations.

Another systematic mistake that a dog can pick up, is if the odors of the foils are systematically laid out first, and the matching odor is added last. Dogs are sensitive to time and concentration differences, it appears they find the direction in a track by noticing differences in concentration between one footstep and the other. If the matching odor is systematically added to the line-up last, this can also be a cue a dog learns to use.

A systematic mistake often is seen in detector dogs like in search and rescue dogs where dogs always choose the easiest way to come to their 'find'. All search dogs prefer to use the track or trail of someone who laid out the scent or 'victims' in a room or building or even outside. Instructors of detector dogs and also search and rescue dogs should prevent dogs using such 'footprint highways' to come to their goal f.i. by laying a lot of tracks with more people.

In training, it is important to avoid these kind of systematic mistakes, since the dog can use them. While we then think the dog is working well, he is in fact using quite different cues than we want him to use. A slightly different procedure brings this to light, and once we discover the dogs have learnt to use another cue we are thrown way back in training.

Handling Mistakes

A dog must continue to search in spite of a verbal correction. If a dog becomes nervous, he is not searching well anymore but primarily paying attention to its handler. For an important part the basic trust between dog and handler must be built up outside of the search work training. A mistake made in search work is not self-rewarding since the dog is not rewarded. This makes it possible to correct the dog verbally softly. If a dog reacts strongly to vocal corrections, it is possible to use a very thin leash and correct the dog with a small jerk. In this case the dog has to get used to working on a leash, and this needs to be done in simple search work until the dog is completely accustomed to the leash and is not hindered by it in any way. Only then can the leash be used for corrections.

Chapter 7

'Shape' and 'Content' Problems

A number of general training problems can occur when training search dogs. These can be divided roughly into 'shape' and 'content' problems. 'Shape' problems are problems with the manner (technique) in which the search work is performed; 'content' problems are problems with making correct matches.

When there are 'shape' problems that need to be solved, the general rule is to make the recognition for the dog (the 'content') very easy. This means offering a choice at a lower level of training than what the dog is already capable of.

The reason for this is that when a handler corrects or influences his dog, the attention of the dog will focus on his handler. This means that he will not be paying as much attention to the scent as he should be in order to make a recognition.

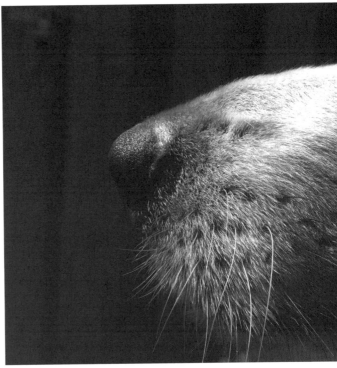

For good scent perception, practice is especially important - both physically and mentally. Regular exposure to training-scents leads to physical changes in the olfactory organ that increases the sensitivity for these scents.

To prevent an association between 'difficult' recognitions and handler influence, and to ensure that the dog focuses his attention on the scent again as quickly as possible, it is important to let the work be an easy one for the dog. The reverse is also true: if a dog has 'content' difficulties and cannot make certain recognitions, a handler should pay less attention to 'shape' elements and reward the dog more quickly than usual, for example.

183

Reading The Dog

For a search dog handler, the most important parts of his dog's behavior are the acts and body expressions the dog shows while searching. Because this behavior is very complex, we see a whole range of expressions and body language. To read the dog, it is particularly important, that the handler pays attention to all the changes the dog shows in his behavior. For that, of course, one has to know the dog thoroughly in normal situations, at home as well as during training. That requires a long and close cooperation, with which one observes the dog continually.

In search work an alert is how the dog makes it clear to his handler that he has located, for instance, by barking, laying down, sitting etc. But most of the time we can also recognize his found by a certain characteristic behavior of the dog. Depending on the time span and the degree of difficulty of the search action, his 'trained alert' can become more weaken. It is very important that every search dog handler is able to read his dog's body language really well. Even after a long search under often stressful circumstances, this is still the alert the dog will show. A dog can be indicating, or at least be finding the scent he is searching for, if:

- the dog, during searching, suddenly changes direction, makes a curve, or so to speak deviates more or lesss from a straight line.
- he changes his tempo, becoming slower or faster.
- he shows interest in a specific area of the search for somewhat longer, also if he is not directly achieving results.
- he stands still somewhere, staring at a certain spot, or 'pointing' like a hunting dog, standing with one of his legs off the ground and looking.
- he begins to scratch or to bite at a particular spot in order to take away pieces of covering material. When, however, a dog only scratches once or a few times, he hasn't ordinarily found the right place. Be careful then and keep quiet, because the dog is still orienting himself.
- the dog tries by intentional movements to bring his handler to the scent clue. Most of the time they behave excited and they make it clear to the handler, by walking there and back, which direction he has to come.

Chapter 7

Training Advice

Performing search work has to be the nicest possible activity for a dog with his handler.

It is obvious that we do not know everything there is to know as yet about the sense of smell, and that it is impossible to objectively determine what a scent is. Even so it is possible to give a few points of attention for training dogs on scents. The points below are valid for all kinds of scent detection training.

• Check if your dog is able to do 'it' at the moment that you really need him. The physical ability to smell varies in time, and the motivation of a dog to work can also vary. It is sensible to check the capacity of your dog: either shortly before, during, or immediately after a practical case.

- Be aware of the phenomenons of adaptation (and cross-adaptation). This may make it impossible for the dog to locate the source of a smell, since the environment is already satiated with the smell. Adjust your training and search method to this.
- Be aware that differences in amount of scent can be perceived as differences in kind of scent. Train on small, but also on large amounts, and do not expect immediate success: if a dog can find a small amount it does not automatically mean he will also be able to find a large amount.
- Practice is for scent perception especially important, both physically and mentally. Regular exposure to training-scents leads to physical changes in the olfactory organ that increases the sensitivity for these scents.
- Learning things young, makes life easy. Scents learned when young are remembered extremely well. By beginning early (perhaps even in the litter) this process is used effectively.
- First train on single scents, later on complexes of scents. This speeds up the learning process.
- It is not possible to always prevent mistakes. The influence of a scent on the behavior of a dog through the limbic system and possible interactions of a scent with memories can lead to all sorts of unpredicted effects. Try, where possible, to find out why things happen and then use this information in training.
- Most of the above points are also valid for scent identification training. However, there is a principle difference: in scent identification line-up training the dog must continuously match odors and not to memorize particular scents. This matching of odors is a far more difficult paradigm than detection, and this in turn has particular consequences for the selection of appropriate dogs.
- It is advantageous to work in a group and to discuss problems prior to doing something about them. Others often see things a handler himself has not yet noticed. Discussing and thoroughly analyzing a problem often leads to a direct solution.

Chapter 8:
Avoiding and Preventing Fraud

In former chapters of this book we discussed the different ways fraud can be commited by handers for police dogs. In this chapter we want to inform about the possibilities of avoiding and preventing fraud. We will do this by discussing the different causes of fraud, such as:

1. Unintentional fraud.
2. Intentional fraud.
3. Use of civilians in criminal investigation.
4. Contamination of scents.
5. Improper training.
6. Unfamiliarity with humans influencing dogs.

Scent Identification Line-Ups

To return to the story of the first chapter, in the appeal case in 2006 – the court in the Dutch town of Leeuwarden decided to start an investigation against the scent identification line-up dog team. This was largely due to the false evidence of which two suspects of a robbery were convicted by the lower court to forty and thirty months imprisonment. In examination in court, the dog handler declared that the scent line-ups were not done in accordance with the protocol. One of the rules says that the scent identification line-up has to be worked out 'blind,' which means that the dog handler doesn't know which place

In the Netherlands, a certified helper places the stainless steel scent carriers on the platforms while the dog and it's handler are absence. (KLPD, 2002)

on the platform contains the tubes with the odor of the suspect.

This was brought about because the helper forgot to clean the blackboard. In order to avoid such fraud, a helper, a police officer who prepares the scent line-up, first writes the lay-out scheme of the different tubes on a blackboard. After, it is in the rules that the helper is to wipe this scheme off the blackboard before the dog handler enters the room. This must happen in order to avoid the dog handler from gaining the foreknowledge, and by that influencing the dog.

Based on this information, the court could do nothing else but excluding the scent identification line-up, and because there was almost no evidence the suspects were acquitted of this charge. Immediately after that the National Department of Criminal Investigation started an investigation against both policemen. Both had testified in the official report that 'the dog handler wasn't acquainted with the positions of the tubes on the platform,' which was signed by both officers. This fraudulent action could have easily been avoided by working more careful and keep to the rules of the scent identification line-up protocol.

1. Unintentional Fraud

- *Negligent treatment*

By sloppy and hasty work a lot of faults are made. In the scent identification line-up, this starts with the installing of the scent carriers at the platform by the helper. If this does not happen carefully and in accordance to the rules, glaring and inexcusable errors occur. This can also happen if the dog handler works too hasty and places pressure on his dog to perform. That is also often seen in tracking, following the scent traces of human footprints. Mistakes occur by carelessness and contamination of scents and footprints. This can easily happen in cases of mantrailing, where the corpus delicti is used to give the dog scent to follow.

- *Not keeping to the protocol*

As soon as the rules and protocols have been abandoned, mistakes come into being. Not working according to the protocol will result in a defence attorney to quickly have the evidence excluded as proof from the case.

Management Attention

Managers of scent identification units need to be aware of the 'scoring positive identifications' and 'number of cases' pitfalls. It is essential that whoever manages the unit realizes all of the aspects that influence the reliability of the line-ups, and focuses on the right quality parameters. The focus should be on quality, not quantity.

The percentage of operational line-ups where a dog has made a positive

Management should focus on controllable quality parameters for their dog handlers.

identification has limited value. If, within a group of dogs that all perform the same kind of line-ups, a certain dog performs much less than the other dogs, this may be something to look at more closely. It may mean that this dog requires more training, or that it fails in the final step. Some insight can be gained by presenting this dog with duplicate line-ups where the result of other dogs was positive. But comparing the percentage positive identifications between dogs who work in geographically different areas, and thus with material and suspects collected by different police investigative teams, does not necessarily say much about a difference in quality of the dogs involved. Perhaps the police teams have very different attitudes towards scent identification line-ups, one team requesting them to support the admission of a suspect, the other team seeing them as a last resort when everything else has failed (and they may be looking at an innocent person.) The areas could also differ in the quality of the scent traces that are being collected and stored.

Management should not focus on positive identifications as a quality parameter, and certainly not demonstrate enthusiasm for a high percentage 'positive identifications.' This is potentially dangerous for the reliability of the line-ups. Management should also be careful in judging the scent identification teams on the number of cases the dogs are being used in.

Management should focus on controllable quality parameters. Thus, the percentage of recognitions in controlled trials should be as high as possible, and the percentage of mistakes should be as low as possible. All dogs make mistakes. If these parameters reach impossible heights one should look more carefully.

By analyzing the use of the line-ups, improvements can be made in the procedures that are followed, or in the information that is given to all relevant parties. For example, we now see that in the Netherlands the courts are paying more and more attention to the correct collection and registration of the scent traces. Too often, the official documentation on this part of the process lacks the necessary detail. By timely informing the police officers involved, this mistake can be adjusted before it leads to the devaluation of scent identification line-ups as a whole.

Managers therefore also have to inform the complete judicial system of the relevance and reliability of scent identification line-ups. They need to be aware of what a scent identification line-up is: establishing, with a given reliability, an odor link between an object and a suspect. They also need to know that there are regulations to be met, and how to check these. They need to realize that this odor link is part of a chain of evidence: the object itself needs to be linked to the crime. They need to know the differences in reliability between 'odor recognition' and 'no odor match'.

It is important, when informing members of the judicial system, to match the information level to the audience. Thus, all police officers informing the judicial members need to follow a professional approach, and accept the limitations of what dogs can do. Claiming: 'My dog never makes a mistake' disqualifies the speaker as a serious professional since everyone realizes this is impossible!

2. Intentional fraud

- *Intentionally work up to a certain result*

Normally there is no cure for intentional fraud. But a proper quality control system – with videotaping for example – of the dog and handler's performances can, in a lot of cases, find possible fraud. Did they follow exactly the protocol and are departures of it mentioned in the official report of the case?

- *Financial benefit*

From certain cases in the past we know that dog handlers were involved in cases that provided monitary compensation if they achieve a certain result. Again, a good control system can avoid fraudulent handling.

- *Faster or easier 'solved' cases*

If the pressure of work is too high, a dog handler may try to solve a case as quickly or as easily as possible without concerning about the real result of that case. This, of course can also happen in order to get more time off for the dog handler.

- *Disguise the characteristics of the dog*

A dog may be certified, even if it has a lower level of performance. In more difficult cases the dog cannot bring the results, and fails. In order to diguise it a dog handler can 'interfere' and 'adjust' the performance of his dog in a certain direction.

- *Become known in the media*

Much more than in former times the media is looking over the shoulders of criminal investigators, and that way also the performances of handlers and dogs. We can see their names and picture in the press and on television. Some handlers may 'solve' as many cases as possible with their dogs to become famous in the media.

- *Being a better dog handler then others*

In a team of dog handlers there can be a keen but sound competition in training the best dogs. As soon as it becomes an 'unhealthy' competition a dog handler can be tempted to fraud in order to continue performing well.

Chapter 8

An explosive case

A case of intentional fraud occurred in the state of Virginia in 2003. D.A. Smith wrote about this case. Russell Ebersole, a dog trainer from Stephenson, near Winchester, had a dog training business named 'Detector Dogs Against Drugs and Explosives.' He got $700 000 to train twenty three explosive detector dogs for the Federal Government. But he was exposed as a fraud after his 'trained' explosive detector dogs were tested by someone in the government. Ebersole's dogs guarded numerous governmental buildings in and around Washington D.C. and there were five test conducted. Two of these tests happened with cars in which fifty pounds (over twenty kilograms) of dynamite was transported, and in the other car were fifty pounds (over twenty kilograms) of plastic explosives. These cars were driven through the checkpoints of buildings Ebersole's dogs were guarding. None of the twenty three dogs found the explosives. The failure of the dogs to detect the explosives was investigated and revealed that Ebersole faked the dog's and handler's certifications and lied about the handler's training. He was arrested for twenty six cases of fraud and forgery, and eventually convicted and sentenced to eighteen years in prison and ordered to repay $700 000 to the Federal Government.

3. Civilians in Crimal Investigations

'I have never seen civilians that came to a crime scene searching for blood traces, fingerprints, DNA, cartridges or pointed weapons, because they thought they could do better than the forensic investigators.'

- *Is their help necessary or do they intrude?*

Conspicuous is the way in which civilian dog handlers think they have to behave in order to twart a criminal investigation. I never saw civilians that came to a crime scene searching for blood traces, fingerprints, DNA, cartridges or pointed weapons, because they thought they could do better than the forensic investigators. But, as soon as police is searching with police dogs, or on the contrary decides not to search with their dogs for technical reasons (for instance the tracks are too old), a lot of the time civilians with their dogs want to take over the investigation. This especially happens in cases of missing people. In those cases, police cannot exclude to possibility of a crime, and for that reason doesn't want to get in civilians involved, such handlers of search and rescue dogs, tracking dogs or mantrailing dogs contact the family and offer their help. And they don't hesitate in the press or on television to criticize the police for not accepting their help, because they find themselves the only specialist for searching.

- *Civilian dogs certified by correct standards?*

Of course it is important that if civilians and their search and rescue dogs, tracking dogs or mantrailing dogs are used in investigations, that they meet the same standards as used for police K9's, and can demonstrate this by passed examinations.

- *A missing persons case can become a crime*

A lot of cases are known to be initially just a missing person case, but after some investigation becomes a criminal offence. In that case it is very important that civilians and their dogs withdraw from the scene and leave the case to forensic investigators. Several times in the past this was rather difficult, because the civilians didn't want to give up searching, didn't want to leave the search areas and thus thwart the police work.

- *Prepared to recognize certain traces of crime?*

A lot of search and rescue groups, just like civilians with trackers or mantrailers, walk in areas like a bull in a china shop without concerning themselves that the missing of a person can become a criminal act. Therefore in training, such civilians should be practiced in recognizing signs and marks that indicate a crime could have taken place.

Shady Evidence

On September 13, 2003, the eleven-years-old Shakira Johnson left her parental home in Cleveland, Ohio, on her way to a party where she never arrived. On October 15, after an anonymous tip-off the police found her already strongly decomposed nude body in a weed-strewn field about a mile and a half from her house. The inquest proved that at the day of her vanish she was sexually assaulted and killed. Soon Daniel Hines, 26, a learning-disabled handyman from Cleveland, was suspected and arrested. Hines had recently been released on bail after a sexual assault charge involving his cousin.

More than thirty days after she vanished, the FBI asked for assistance of a Bloodhound.

After the body of Shakira was found, more than 30 days after she vanished, the FBI asked for assistance of a Bloodhound. At the place were the body was discovered the dog found a 'track', followed it, but soon lost it. But the Bloodhound 'scented' Shakira's odor also at two other locations. One location was in the bathroom of a house Hines shared with his family, so a place a lot of people went in and out. The other place where the Bloodhound 'alerted' to Shakira's scent was at the passenger side door of Hine's van which was stored at a police impound lot. But the strange thing about this is that a police report showed they attempted to do this same thing a month earlier with two dogs and the result was 'negative.' It was after this first attempt, they returned the van and then re-seized it some time later before the Bloodhound.

The judge in this case ruled that the dog handler would not be allowed to testify because there were no eyewitnesses who corroborated that Shakira had been in Hines' van or home. Hines' attorneys argued the dog handler's testimony was unreliable, and the seven women and five men of the jury on December 19, 2004 acquitted Daniel Hines of kidnapping and murdering Shakira Johnson.

4. Contamination of scents

• *Dual-purpose trained dogs*

Here dual-purpose means dogs trained for detecting human odor as well as drugs, or explosives. This, for instance, was a fault in the 'Fitting-room Murder Case' as was written in chapter one. Police dog 'Tim' who did the scent identification line-up was also trained as a drug detector dog. And the bicycle dealer who in the line-up was identified by the dog in that time really used drugs sometimes.

• *Keep and use scent and objects clean*

It is very important that odors are conserved in a correct way, without contamination with other scents. Also in using and offering the scents to the dog one must be very careful not to contact scents with possible other scents. Cleaning procedures are required after use of tubes and glass jars. They are either sterilized in a stove, or they are washed with soap in a dishwasher that is only used for that task, prior to being boiled in clean water.

Chapter 8

- *Clean-scent training*

If we want a dog to become interest a certain scent, we always train him by offering that scent as pure as possible and enough of the sent for it to perceptived. This means that in line-ups the scent of the person that has to be detected on the platform must be offered to the dog without any 'mixing' with other scents. Also in teaching clean-scent tracking (see Gerritsen & Haak, 2001) the dog must track only the meaningfull scented articles of the tracklayer. And, of course, the 'scent article' a dog initially scents when beginning a trail in mantrailing only has the odor of the person that walks the trail.

Making impossible possible

Be very careful when using civilians for police tasks - even in 'missing persons' cases.

We again will underline that we have nothing against Bloodhounds or working with Bloodhounds. In Europe as well as in America, there are a lot of good and very honest working police dog handlers that understand the limits of their dogs to percept scents, and they will not cross those borders. If such a border for the dog comes into being, such as because the scent is too old, they will accept that and grant.

No, we raise an objection to those police dog handlers who sometimes unintentional, but a lot of times very intentional, try to make impossibilities possible. Where honest dog handlers stop, others go on and commit fraud in order to be in the right. This is a complete discredit the honest and truthful police dog handlers. The only thing they want is to be in the right and 'steal the show' with their dog.

But there is more!

A lot of good police dog handlers are criticized by their superiors or civil servants, because their dogs cannot perform the things such fraudulent handlers say they can with their dogs. Such superiors hear or read these spectacular results and ask their dog handlers 'Why can't do our dogs such things?'

Well, we hope we have shown in this book that fraudulent dog handlers cannot perform such spectacular things! Here are some tips from D.A. Smith for the superiors to find out what kind of dog handler you meet:

- First, check all the backgrounds and the certifications of handlers and dogs. Ask for certification from a national police dog association.
- Be very careful with claims that a dog can do something other police dogs cannot.
- Be very careful using civilians for police tasks; also check all the backgrounds and the certifications of handlers and dogs. And check if the certifications and judges of the exams are by the same standards as used for police dogs.
- Also in 'missing person cases' be careful using civilians which are not trained in recognizing signs and marks that indicate a crime.
- Most civilians are not trained in evidence preservation or court testimony.

A lot of good police dog handlers are criticized by their superiors because their dogs cannot perform the things fraudulent handlers say they can with their dogs.

5. Improper training

• *Easy scoring by using tracks*

For a start, be aware of the pitfall that dogs always choose the easiest way to come to their 'find.' Know that all search dogs prefer to use the track or trail of someone who laid out the scent or scent articles in a room or building or even outside. Instructors of detector dogs and also search and rescue dogs should prevent dogs using such 'footprint highways' to come to their goal. This can be prevented by laying a lot of tracks with more people during training.

- *Selection of starting material*

Training can only lead to success if the starting material is good. So, we have to look carefully at the characteristics of the dog we want to train. But it is equally important to look at the characteristics of the handler who is going to teach the dog, and to look at the kind of team the handler and his dog become. Scent training is mentally the most challenging kind of training. It requires a stable adult mentality of both the dog and its handler.

Of course, it is very necessary to have a healthy dog. Many kinds of illnesses and medication affect the nose. Training the dog while his sense of smell is not optimal will lead to all kinds of unnecessary stress situations that are detrimental to the training. The physical characteristics of a good dog are:

- Complete health and sound in life and limb;
- Easy and fast movements;
- Strong and muscled body;
- Good sense of smell, sight and hearing;
- Good and powerful mouth;
- Optimal condition and very strong stamina;
- Strong legs, and feet with strong soles;
- Adapted to the weather and climate in which he has to work;
- A fur coat suitable for that purpose.

Scent dog training requires very intensive mental work. It is the most difficult activity to a traditional dog in terms of cognitive abilities. So it requires a stable, adult mentality of both dog and handler.

The mental characteristics of a potentially good dog are:

- Placid composure: self confident, stable, not nervous or afraid;
- Temperament: lively, interested;
- Willing to work: willingness to continue even if there is no immediate reward;
- Intelligence: a high practical intelligence and good adaptive intelligence. We distinguish between three forms of intelligence. Namely the instinctive,

the practical and the adaptive intelligence. By instinctive intelligence we mean all hereditary skills and behavior. For instance, the hunting drive – every puppy runs after a moving object. By practical intelligence we mean the speed with which, and the degree to which, the dog conforms to the desires of the handler. Roughly said, how quickly and how correctly the dog learns the different exercises. Adaptive intelligence can be divided into two abilities: learning proficiency, which means how quickly the dog develops adequate behavior in new situations, and the problem solving ability. This last is the dog's skill to choose the correct behavior to solve a problem he encounters.
- Good searching drive: natural ability to use the nose to find objects;
- Not too high prey drive: if the dog defends his reward too strongly, he will be focused on the reward itself too much and this will prevent him from searching well;
- High bring drive: by retrieving his reward to his handler, the dog shares it with him and this is good for the team;
- Ability to cope with mistakes: if corrected (a verbal correction should be sufficient), the dog should remain composed, willing to work, and not lose its search and bring drive. Dogs that cannot cope quickly with being corrected are very difficult to work with.

These are characteristics only found in mature dogs. Although training can begin before puberty, we have not found this to significantly shorten the training time or to increase the final performance level. Preparing a dog for scent tasks should include a good socialization; teaching him general obedience, and stimulating his search and bring drive through games. Here, care should be taken that the dog learns to search with his nose. This is the kind of behavior we want him to have later, and the active use of the nose enhances its development, ensuring a good starting-point.

- *The team: handler and dog*
Some of these characteristics will develop during the training, and cannot be fully tested beforehand. One can try to test the will to work, for example, but

finally the dog will have to maintain this will to work in performing special scent tasks. This may make a difference. The ability to cope with mistakes is another characteristic one cannot really test beforehand, but it has proven to be very important.

A handler must also have a stable character and not be easily agitated by his dog's behavior. He must have learned to interpret the behavior of different dogs, and be able to read their signals quickly. He must have a lot of patience, be willing to review his own training critically, and go a step back in training regularly. He must be very aware of the possible pitfalls he can come across in this work, especially the Clever Hans kind of problems. This means that he has to accept that it is good if the dog does not pay very much attention to him, which is quite different from normal obedience work. He must realize that the dog is the only one who can smell well enough to solve the problem. He must never try to force his dog into 'alerting a scent clue' but try to adapt his training to maneuver the dog into understanding what is expected of him. In short, he must be an intelligent and sensitive trainer who stays ahead of his dog one step all the time.

An inadequate handler can ruin a potentially good dog. A good handler can go quite a long way with a not-so-good dog, but he will not be able to achieve the high standard necessary for operational work. So it is best to first look at the handler critically, and in terms of dogs: if things do not go well, stop. It is very important that the handler likes the dog he works with and that there are no tensions between them: neither during training, but also not outside of the training. And it is important that activities outside of the scent training suit the dog and the handler and should improve their relationship, not creating tension. If there is stress between the handler and his dog, it will show up in the scent training and play an important, negative role.

- ***Unsuitable dog for the task***

A good selection of dog can prevent training for special police tasks from starting with unsuitable circumstances. It can happen that the dog in question itself has less qualities – but it can also happen that a dog has to fit in a certain training method regardless of their physiological or mental abilities, because the handler or instructor has command of only one training method.

- ### *Use of an incorrect training method*
A good dog handler (and instructor) knows several training methods and is well informed about all new developments in dog training. Only in that way he can always adopt the best fitting training method to a certain dog, in order to get the best results with that dog. Every dog is unique and for that needs a certain way of training. We always are surprised to see how some dog handlers or instructors only know one method of training and try to fit that to all their dogs. There the dog has to be adapted to that method instead of fitting a method to the dog, and their results most of the time are not up to the mark.

- ### *Too fast to get results*
A very big problem in training police dogs for a special task can be due to the shortness of training time availible, by which dogs have to learn exercises under pressure and stress. Just like people, dogs need time to mentally deal with new exercises or circumstances. Of course, this can happen because of a short training period, but we are very sorry to say that we know dog handlers rushing through the training in order to free up time for themselves.

- ### *Dog's physical, mental and search condition*
The physical, the mental and the search condition in dogs interact and exert a great influence on the achievements of the dog. It is correct to declare that here.

Physical condition: Dogs must have proper and well-trained muscles and optimal state of the body of the dog. The dog must be fed proper foods. When this is lacking, we see physical exhaustion after a brief exertion. With poor or insufficient feeding we see that hunger dominates, and that causes lack of concentration, insufficient energy to perform and intense nervousness.

Mental condition: Dogs must be able to perform by themselves, and with enthusiasm when working out the exercise, without pressure or compulsion of the handler. When lacking, we see apathy or just great stress; also physical tiredness.

Search condition: Search dogs are required the ability to keep concentration long enough to work out the scent work. When lacking, we see dogs which need a break after a short time because of concentration problems.

- *Are the examination requirements realistic?*

The examination requirements for police dogs have to be at such a high level that professional work with the dog can be guaranteed. In the highest examinations for sport tracking dogs, tracks of 1 800 meters in length and three hours old have to be worked out, and in mantrailing much longer and older trails.

Search and rescue dog handlers should be practiced in recognizing signs and marks in 'missing cases' that indicate a crime could have taken place.

So we are very astonished at reading a test for police search dogs in which a less realistic track of about thousand metres and about one hour old is required.

Insurance Fraud

To conclude the examples of deceit mentioned in this book here is a very special case of fraud with a policedog. In Oakland, about fifty kilometers from Memphis, Tennessee a case of insurance fraud with a police dog came in court. The former Oakland police chief Bob Tisdale and two former Oakland officers, Herbert Brewer and Billy Allen Usselton, were indicted on charges of faking the death of a police dog named Kit in 2004, then collecting the $5 000 insurance policy for the town. Kit was reportedly killed during training in Hardeman County. Four years later, authorities received information that the dog was alive, leading to an inquiry by the Tennessee Bureau of Investigations, that later announced Kit was found living in Tipton County. Tisdale pleaded guilty, got three years probation and pay $1 666.66 in restitution (his share after being divided between the two other defendants) for the police dog.

6. Unfamiliar influences on dogs

- ***Handlers, instructors, helpers and spectators***

All through this book we have indicated that dogs are very quick to react on even minor cues we, sometimes unconscious of, give to them. Such slight signs are called 'Clever Hans' cues, based on the ability to count by tapping his. Hans responded to the slight cues of his owner leaning forward to stop tapping his hoof when he had reached the correct answer.

Influencing of the dog by the handler, just as by instructors, helpers and spectators, still is an important object in dog training. Dogs learn very fast to react on people present that know where something or someone is hidden. The only way to avoid such Clever Hans clues is, as soon as the dog understands the technique of tracking or searching, to work 'blind', that means don't know the position of the track or the hiding place.

K9 Fraud!

'Blind' tracking means that the dog handler is all alone with his dog, and there is nobody in the neighberhood who knows the path of the track and by that can influence the tracking...

- **Training 'controlled' or really 'blind'?**

A lot of dog handlers think that they track blind, because they don't know the path of the track. But the tracklayer, or instructor who knows the track, walks close behind the dog handler, and the last trusts that the tracklayer will interfere if things go wrong. And also the dog learns after a few tracks to listen to the footsteps, voice and breathing of the tracklayer. So this is not 'blind' tracking, but 'controlled' tracking!

Really 'blind' tracking means that the dog handler is all alone with his dog, and there is nobody in the neighberhood who knows the path of the track and so can influence the tracking. In really 'blind' tracking the dog handler knows nothing, except the place where he has to start (near a tree, car, footprint, etc.), and comes back with the articles found at the track and/or the tracklayer who was sitting or laying at the end of the track.

This difference between 'controlled' and 'blind' working can also be seen in detector dogs searching for drugs, explosives, arson or in search and rescue dogs underneath the rubble hidden persons. Also there the helper who hided the substances or persons, just like the instructor, stays in the same room where the dog has to search. Most of the time with their faces to the hiding place. Dogs learn by itself unerringly to stay searching in the surrounding of these persons, because they noted that the helper and instructor always wanted to see the dog's alert.

If the handler and dog are too far away from the hiding place they normally can read that from the position or the attention of the helper and/or instructor. If the last persons suddenly stop talking the handler may conclude that he, but for sure his dog, comes close to the scent spot. So also here we can speak of 'controlled' searching.

Because real 'blind' searching happens only if the helper or instructor indicates a number of rooms, objects or buildings in which may be the handler and his dog can have a find. There, all by himself the handler has to show he can work with his dog as a team, and only then it is really exciting, and very realistic!

K9 Fraud!

Bibliography

American Bloodhound Club, 2009. Trailing Trial Event Standard. Revised December 2001. http://www.bloodhounds.org/trailing/trailingstandard.pdf

Belleville, R., 1938. Neue Versuche auf dem Gebiet der Fährtenarbeit und des Identifizierens von Gegenständen auf der Fährte. Zeitschrift für Hundeforschung, Band XIII, 17-28.

Blunk, R., 1926. Die Ausbildung des Hundes zur Spurenreinheit. Hinstorff, Rostock.

Bodingbauer, J., 1977. Das Wunder der Hundenase. Unsere Hunde, Wien.

Boyse, E.A., 1986. HLA and the chemical senses. Human Immunology, 15: 391-395.

Briewasser, I., 1989. Fährtenarbeit, die Grenze der Belastbarkeit. Unsere Hunde, January.

Brisbin Jr, I.L. and Austad, S.N., 1991. Testing the individual odour theory of canine olfaction. Animal Behaviour 42: 63-69.

Brough, E., 1905. The Bloodhound and its use in tracking criminals. Illustrated Kennel News, London.

Bryson, S., 2000. Police Dog Tactics. Detselig Enterprises Ltd., Calgary, Canada.

Budgett, H.M., 1933. Hunting by Scent. Charles Scribner, New York.

Buytendijk, F.J.J., 1932. De psychologie van den hond. Kosmos, Amsterdam.

Casey, R., 2009. Dog's nose fallible as a crime lab. Houston Chronicle, June 30.

Clifford, R.J., 1958. Some notes and theories on scent, its formation, properties and usage as derived from observations on and experience with tracker and patrol dogs. J.R. Arm. Vet. Corps 29: 145.

Fox, M.W., 1971. Behaviour of wolves, dogs and related canids. Jonathan Cape, London.

Frawley, E., 2000. Bloodhounds. Website: http://leerburg.com/bloodhound.htm

Frawley, E., 2002. Bloodhounds & Baloney. Website: http://leerburg.com/bloodhounds.htm

Gerritsen, R. and Haak, R., 1999. K9 Search and Rescue, A New Training Method. Detselig Enterprises Ltd., Calgary, Canada.

Gerritsen, R. and Haak, R., 2001. K9 Professional Tracking: A complete manual for theory and training. Detselig Enterprises Ltd., Calgary, Canada.

Haak, R., 1986. Het speuren van honden in theorie en praktijk. Zuidboek, Best.

Haak, R., 2006. De neus van de hond. Bloemendal Uitgevers bv, Amersfoort.

Hansmann, J., 1931. Unter welchen Gesichtspunkten erfolgt die praktische Verwendung des Polizeifährtenhundes? Zeitschrift für Hundeforschung I, 14-30.

Honhon, J., 1967. l'Olfaction chez le Chien. Son rôle dans le pistage et la localisation d'une source odorante. Dissertation, Paris.

Innocence Project, 2009. Know the Cases & Unvalidated or Improper Forensic Science. Website: http://www.innocenceproject.org

Innocence Project of Texas, 2009. Dog Scent Lineups, A Junk Science Injustice. A Special Report. September 21. Website: http://ipoftexas.org

Katz, D., 1947. Animals and Man. Longmans Green & Co., London.

Krall, K., 1912. Denkende Tiere, Beitrage zur Tierseelenkunde auf Grund eigener Versuche, der Kluge Hans und meine Pferde Muhamed und Zarif. Friedrich Engelman, Leipzig.

Lavandera, E., 2009. Dogs sniff out wrong suspect; scent lineups questioned. CNN.com/crime. 05-10.

Ledden Hulsebosch, C.J. v., 1940. Veertig Jaren Speurderswerk. Kemink en Zoon N.V., Utrecht.

Löhner, L., 1924. Über menschliche Individual- und Regionalgerüche. Arch. Ges. Physiol. 202, 25-45.

Menzel, R. and R., 1930. Die Verwertung der Riechfähigkeit des Hundes im Dienste der Menschheit. Kameradschaft-Verlag, Berlin.

Miklósi, Á., Polgárdi, R., Topál, J. and Csányi, V., 1998. Use of experimenter-given cues in dogs. Animal Cognition 1: 113-121.

Miller M. and Klaidman D., 2002. Hunt for the Anthrax Killer. Newsweek Magazine, August 12.

Moncrieff, R.W., 1967. The Chemical Senses. Leonard Hill, London, 730 pp.

Most, K., 1926. Neue Versuche über Spürfähigkeit. Z.D. Hund Nr. 18., 31-35.

Most, K. and Brückner, G.H., 1936. Über Voraussetzungen und den derzeitigen Stand der Nasenleistungen von Hunden. Zeitschrift für Hundeforschung. Heft 5, 9-30.

Moxley, R.S., 2005. The Case of the Dog That Couldn't Sniff Straight. OC Weekly, 03-11.

Mynsinger, H., 1473. Puoch von den valken, habichten, sperbern, pfaeriden, und hunden. In: M. von Stephanitz, Der deutsche Schäferhund in Wort und Bild, Anton Kampfe, Jena.

Neuhaus, W., 1953. Über die Riechschärfe des Hundes für Fettsäuren. Zeitschrift für vergleichende Physiologie, Bd. 35, 527-552.

Neuhaus, W., 1955. Die Unterscheidung von Duftquantitäten bei Mensch und Hund nach

Versuchen mit Buttersäure. Zeitschrift für vergleichende Physiologie, Bd. 37: 234-252.

NEUHAUS, W., 1956. Die Unterscheidungsfähigkeit des Hundes für Duftgemische. Zeitschrift für vergleichende Physiologie, Bd. 39, 25-43.

NEUHAUS, W., 1981. Die Bedeutung des Schnüffelns für das Riechen des Hundes. Zeitung für Säugetierkunde. Bd. 46, 301-310.

NICKEL, R., SCHUMMER A. AND SEIFERLE E., 1984. Lehrbuch der Anatomie der Haustiere. Band IV. Nervensystem, Sinnesorgane, Endokrine Drüsen. Paul Parey, Berlin.

PFUNGST, O., 1911. Clever Hans. The horse of Mr. Von Osten. Holt, Rinehart & Winston, New York.

PONGRÁCZ, P., MIKLÓSI, A., KUBINYI, E., GUROBI, K., TOPÁL, J. AND CSÁNYI, V., 2001. Social learning in dogs: the effect of a human demonstrator on the performance of dogs in a detour task. Animal Behaviour, 62, 1109-1117.

RITEA, S., 2002. Dogs to aid search for B.R. serial killer. Capital bureau/The Times-Picayune, 21.09.

ROMANES, G.J., 1887. Experiments on the sense of smell in dogs. Nature 36: 273-274.

RAMOTOWSKI, R.S., 2001. Composition of latent fingerprint residue. In: Advances in Fingerprint Technology, Ed. H.C. Lee & R.E. Gaensslen, CRC Press, Boca Raton.

SALAZAR, I., BARBER, P.C. AND CIFUENTES, J.M., 1992. Anatomical and Immunohistological Demonstration of the Primary Neural Connections in the Vomeronasal Organ in the Dog. The Anatomical Record 233: 309-313.

SCHMID, B., 1937. Umfang und Grenzen der Nasenleistung von Hunden. Forsch. Fortschr. 13: 26-27.

SCHMIDT, F., 1910. Verbrecherspur und Polizeihund. Selbstverlag SV, Augsburg.

SCHMIDT, F., 1911. Polizeihund-Erfolge und Neue Winke. Selbstverlag SV, Augsburg.

SCHOON, A. AND HAAK R., 2002. K9 Suspect Discrimination: Training and practicing scent identification line-ups. Detselig Enterprises Ltd., Calgary, Canada.

SIBER, M., 1899. Die Hunde Afrikas. St. Gallen.

SMITH, D.A., 2004. Fraudulent Use of Canines in Police Work. School of Police Staff and Command. Eastern Michigan University.

SOBEL, N., KHAN, R., SULLIVAN, E., AND GABRIELI, J.D.E., 2000. The world smells different to each nostril. Nature. 402, 35.

SOPRONI, K., MIKLÓSI, Á., TOPÁL, J. AND CSÁNYI, V., 2001. Comprehension of human communicative signs in pet dogs (Canis familiaris). J. Comp. Psychol. 115(2): 122-126.

Soproni, K., Miklósi, Á., Topál, J. and Csányi, V., 2002. Dog's Responsiveness to human pointing gestures. J. Comp. Psychol. 116(1): 27-34.

Soschtschenko, M., 1929. Remarkable Nose in a Police Dog. De Hond 4: 87-88.

Spielman, A.I. , Zeng, X.N, Leyden, J.J. and Preti, G., 1995. Proteinacceous precursors of human axillary odor: isolation of two novel odor-binding proteins. Experientia 51: 40-47.

Stephanitz, M. von, 1923. Der deutsche Schäferhund in Wort und Bild. Anton Kampfe, Jena.

Syrotuck, W.G., 1972. Scent and the scenting dog. Arner Publications, Westmoreland, NY.

Taslitz, A.E., 1990. Does the Cold Nose Know? The Unscientific Myth of the Dog Scent Lineup. The Hastings Law Journal 42: 15-134.

Thesen, A., Steen, J.B. and Døving, K.B., 1993. Behaviour of Dogs during Olfactory Tracking. Journal of Experimental Biology, 180, 247-251.

Uchida, T., 1953. Proceedings. XIV. Internat. Congr. Zool., 292.

Uexküll, J. v., 1934. Streifzüge durch die Umwelten von Tieren und Menschen. Verständliche Wissenschaft, XXI, Berlin.

Water, J., 1948. De grote daden van politiehond 'Albert'. De Courant-Nieuws van de Dag. Amsterdam.

Wójcikiewicz, J., 2000. Scientific Evidence in Judicial Proceedings. Institute of Forensic Research Publishers, Kraków.

Zell, Th., 1909. Der Polizeihund als Gehilfe der Strafrechtsorgane. Verlag Guttentag, Berlin.

Zuschneid, K., 1973. Die Riechleistung des Hundes. Dissertation, Freie Univ. Berlin.

About the Authors

Ruud Haak with his German Shepherd 'Yes van Sulieseraad' and Malinois 'Google van het Eldenseveld.'

Resi Gerritsen with her Malinois 'Halusetha's All Power' and Malinois 'Google van het Eldenseveld.'

Ruud Haak was born 1947 in Amsterdam, the Netherlands. At the age of thirteen he was training police dogs at his uncle's Security Dog Training Centre, and when he was fifteen he worked after school with his patrol dog (which he trained himself) in the harbor of Amsterdam. Later on he started training his dogs in Schutzhund and I.P.O., and succesfully bred and showed German Shepherd Dogs and Saint Bernards.

He worked as a social therapist in a government clinic for criminal psychopaths, and from his studies in psychology, his interest was also taken by dog behavior and training methods for nose-work: the Tracking Dog (Fährtenhund) and the Search and Rescue Dog.

In the 1970s, with his wife Dr. Resi Gerritsen, a psychologist and jurist, he attended many courses and symposia with their German Shepherd Dogs for Schutzhund, Tracking Dog and SAR dog training in Switzerland, Germany and Austria. In 1979, they started the Dutch Rescue Dog Organization in the Netherlands. With that unit, they attended a lot of operations after earthquakes, gas explosions, and of course lost persons in large wooded or wilderness areas.

In 1990 Ruud Haak and Resi Gerritsen moved to Austria, where they were asked by the Austrian Red Cross to train and select operational rescue and avalanche dogs. They lived for three years at a height of 1 800 meters (6 000 ft.) in the Alps and worked with their dogs in search missions after avalanches.

With their Austrian colleagues, Ruud and his wife Resi developed a new method for training search and rescue dogs. This way of training showed the best results after the big earthquake in Armenia (1988), Japan (1995), the two major earthquakes in Turkey (1999), and the big eartquakes in Algeria and Iran (2003).

Now they live in the Czech Republic near the Austrian border. They are training directors and international judges for the International Red Cross Federation, the United Nations (OCHA), the International Rescue Dog Organisation (IRO) and the Fédération Cynologique Internationale (FCI).

Ruud and Resi also demonstrated that their unique training methods for tracking dogs as well as search and rescue dogs were successful at the Austrian, Czech, Hungarian and World Championships for search and rescue dogs, where both were several times the leading Champions. At the World Championship in Ljubljana, Slowenia, the authors and their team became the 1999 World Champions.

Resi Gerritsen and Ruud Haak have held, all over the world, many symposia and master classes on their unique training methods, which they wrote down in their books:

- K9 Search and Rescue: A new training method
- K9 Schutzhund Training: A manual for tracking, obedience and protection
- K9 Professional Tracking: A complete manual for theory and training
- K9 Personal Protection: A manual for training reliable protection dogs
- K9 Complete Care: A manual for physically and mentally healthy working dogs
- K9 Working Breeds: Characteristics and capabilities
- K9 Behavior Basics: A manual for proven success in operational service dog training and together with Dr. Adee Schoon, Ruud Haak wrote:
- K9 Suspect Discrimination: Training and practicing scent identification line-ups

(all: Detselig Enterprises Ltd., Calgary, Canada).

Ruud Haak is the author of at least thirty dog books in Dutch and German, and since 1979 he has been the editor-in-chief of the biggest Dutch dog magazine, Onze Hond (Our Dog).

More recently he trained drug and explosive detector dogs for the Dutch police and the Royal Dutch Airforce. He also is a visiting lecturer at the Dutch, German and Austrian police dog schools.

At the moment Ruud and Resi are still successfully training their dogs for Search and Rescue, Tracking, Schutzhund and Protection Dog.

You can contact the authors by e-mail at: onzehond@bcm.nl

K9 Fraud!